THE *Ultimate*
BLENDER
COOKBOOK

THE *Ultimate* BLENDER COOKBOOK

Fast, Healthy Recipes for *Every* Meal

REBECCA MILLER FFRENCH

Photography by Justin Lanier

THE COUNTRYMAN PRESS · WOODSTOCK, VT.

Copyright © 2015 by Rebecca Ffrench
Photographs © Justin Lanier
Design by LeAnna Weller Smith

Published by The Countryman Press, P.O. Box 748, Woodstock, VT 05091
Distributed by W. W. Norton & Company, Inc., 500 Fifth Avenue, New York, NY 10110
Printed in United States

The Unltimate Blender Cookbook
978-1-58157-295

10 9 8 7 6 5 4 3 2 1

To my family, who loves a good laugh and great food

And to all blender lovers looking to whir
their way to wholesome meals

Contents

Acknowledgments

Introduction

While working on this book, I was often asked questions like, "Why the blender? Isn't it easier to mix things by hand? Don't you find it hard to clean?" The short answer: No.

The long answer: A blender can greatly assist a home cook with chopping vegetables, mixing marinades for main courses, and literally whipping up a wholesome dessert—all in minutes. A blender makes meal prep quick and easy. It's a helpful tool for turning fresh, local ingredients into healthful meals—and not just liquid ones. You can greatly boost your nutritional intake by adding greens, nuts, and superfoods to your diet on a daily basis. And the best part: Nutritious can equal delicious!

You see, from the third grade the blender was the one appliance that I didn't have to ask permission to use. I was free to create as I pleased. And so I did. And have continued to do so for almost 30 years, developing recipes that give bang for their buck—creative combinations of natural foods that are nutrient-dense, enhance energy, and, most important, come together quickly.

My first forays into blending involved lots of milk shakes and salsas—perfect after-school snacks for the tween years. During my college days, my blender was primarily an ice crusher (and probably saw more alcohol than it should have!). As I matured and got married, my blender took on a more sophisticated role, blending vinaigrettes and pureeing sauces.

Then baby made three and the blender worked tirelessly pulverizing vegetables into healthy, preservative-free mush for our new addition. Along came baby two, and life got even more hectic, but our blender did not give up on us, nor we on it. Its blades still whirred, now accommodating four. We whipped up everything seemingly possible in our blender: crêpes, muffins, meatless burgers, and more.

When the smoothie phenomenon hit, we were already there, blending away. I found ways to incorporate more foods rich in fiber, antioxidants, and heart-friendly fatty acids into every dish.

In these pages, I want to share my love of blending and show how this miraculous machine can effortlessly aid you in the quest for healthier eating. I admit, I'm a food fanatic. I obsess about every bite my family and I ingest. I want each morsel to melt in our mouths, leaving us happy and satisfied. I hope these recipes relay my sense of excitement about food: bright colors, juicy textures, diverse flavors.

Eating should make you feel good—physically *and* socially—and the blender can help get you there . . . fast. It minimizes prep time, allows you to easily make large quantities for a crowd, and truly is a cinch to clean.

You, too, can turn your blender into a kitchen workhorse, making meals a time to recharge, relax, and connect.

Healthy Made Simple

What is the key to successful blending? Fresh, wholesome ingredients. The fresher the produce, grain, nut, or other foodstuff, the truer the flavor and the more complete the nutrition. You are in control of every ingredient you put in the blender, so the result is up to you. You can replace store-bought foods like muffins and soups with homemade, chemical-free equivalents and swap syrupy bottled salad dressings for sugarless blends.

According to the Centers for Disease Control (CDC), only 32.5 percent of Americans eat the recommended two or more servings of fruits per day. The number drops even lower, to 26.3 percent, for those who eat the recommended three or more servings of vegetables per day.* That means a lot of us aren't eating our fruits and veggies!

Enter the blender. Large amounts of fruits and vegetables can be blended to manageable sizes for easy consumption, and the blender's blades break down cell walls of hard-to-digest raw plant-based foods for better absorption.

It may be tempting to load up smoothies with sugar or sauces with cream, but there's no need when blending. Fruits lend sweetness while nuts and healthy oils can create a velvety texture.

This collection of recipes may serve as a user manual for beginning blenders, a

* Centers for Disease Control and Prevention, "State-Specific Trends in Fruit and Vegetable Consumption Among Adults—United States, 2000–2009," *Morbidity and Mortality Weekly Report* (September 10, 2010).

The Ultimate Blender Book

springboard for those looking to incorporate more fruits and vegetables in their diets, or a resource of new ideas for those already proficient with their blenders.

The goal with these recipes is to use the blender to its fullest potential. Its power is uncanny. A vortex is actually created inside the blender jar, which brings me to the second, third, and fourth most crucial elements of blending: Do not overblend, do not overblend, do not overblend. I know I'm being repetitive, but this should become your mantra. I will reiterate it throughout the book, but when a recipe says to pulse, really pulse. It's so tempting to go just a little more, but a few extra seconds of blending and a potato soup can go from satiny smooth to gummy glue. You can always blend more, but it's difficult to reverse the effects of overblending without starting over, so go slowly. Believe me, I've had to start again more than once (my dog is always happy to sop up my mistakes, though; she never seems to mind the texture!).

My hope is that this book helps make the blender your buddy, that you'll see it as an approachable assistant helping you prepare tasty, healthy meals. I also hope these recipes become part of your daily repertoire, essentials you love and go back to again and again. Use the blender to experiment, put good food on the table, and get things done fast, but most of all—have fun with it!

A Word About Blenders

I use a Vitamix Professional Series 750, and I *love* it. To me, it is the Bentley of blenders. I also have an Oster blender and the Ninja Ultima blender. They both do a fine job, but I have a difficult time blending up burgers in the Oster, and the Ninja just doesn't have the power of the Vitamix. Neither grinds nuts and seeds as thoroughly as the Vitamix.

The Blendtec and the Vitamix are extremely comparable. They both work well, it's just what bells and whistles you prefer. Blendtec is slightly more compact and fits nicely under cupboards; Vitamix blenders come with tampers for pushing ingredients toward the blades; some have pulse buttons, but not all do. Take time to comparison shop and you'll find the right fit. Both will do an exceptional job.

That said, power blenders are extremely expensive. The payoff: healthy natural food prepared with little effort. Power blenders are built to last a lifetime. Most of the recipes in this book require a high-speed blender. Smoothies, salad dressings, and marinades will work with conventional blenders, but for those looking to blend up dishes for every meal, you'll need a power machine. Consider the money spent as an investment in your health, your future, your happiness.

CHAPTER 1

Blender Basics

Are you ready to start blending? Incorporating blender recipes into your daily meal plan will make your life easier—and make you feel good too. But where to start?

The first step: Look at your own kitchen. What ingredients do you have on hand? Using the blender has inspired me to think differently about what I keep in my cupboards and fridge. I have slowly added new ingredients to my shelves—lots of seeds, nuts, and whole grains—and stocked my fridge with an array of fresh produce. The blender has inspired me to consume such a wider variety of fruits and vegetables than ever before.

There are also some important techniques to keep in mind when using a blender. Having a light touch and not over-blending is often the key to success. Remember to work with the blender, not against it. The blender does need your assistance sometimes—you're a team. Actually we're a team: you, me, and the blender. So let's get to it and start blending!

A Well-Stocked Blender Kitchen

Essentials at a Glance

IN THE PANTRY

Oils cold-pressed extra-virgin olive oil, cold-pressed extra-virgin coconut oil, aroma-free coconut oil, organic canola or grapeseed oil

Vinegars balsamic, apple cider (Bragg's), white wine, red wine, and rice wine vinegars

Flours white whole wheat, spelt, oat, light buckwheat, almond and coconut flours

Grains old-fashioned rolled oats, brown rice

Legumes lentils, chickpeas, black beans

Nuts and Seeds almonds, pecans, walnuts, cashews, flaxseeds, hemp seeds, pumpkin seeds, chia seeds, quinoa, nut butters

Sweeteners raw honey, maple syrup, dark brown sugar, organic cane sugar, confectioners' sugar

Canned goods coconut milk, fire-roasted tomatoes, artichoke hearts, beans, chipotles in adobe, pumpkin

Carton goods almond milk, organic chicken broth

Spices and such Maldon salt, kosher salt, cinnamon, coriander, cumin, ginger, nutmeg, paprika, red pepper flakes

Baking items baking powder, baking soda, pure vanilla extract, unsweetened cocoa powder, bittersweet chocolate chips, unsweetened coconut, dates, baking spray, xanthan gum

IN THE FRIDGE

Organic eggs, butter, buttermilk, plain yogurt, ricotta cheese, lemons, limes, Dijon mustard, fresh herbs (cilantro, parsley, rosemary, thyme, basil), kale and other leafy greens

IN THE FREEZER

Ice, homemade chicken stock, berries

IN THE PRODUCE BIN

Avocados, onions, garlic, shallots, fresh ginger

The New Blender Kitchen

Some of the ingredients in this book may be new to you—they were to me just a few years back. While my local market carries most ingredients used in this book, when I asked the cashier if they sold chia seeds, she melodically chimed back, "Ch-Ch-Ch-Chia? Aren't those sold on TV with a clay pet?" And even my own mother asked, "Can you get high from hemp seeds?"

Most of these items should be readily available at conventional markets, but you may have to search farther afield to find a natural food store or online retailer.

Budget is a huge consideration when stocking your cupboards with organic, natural staples. Healthy foods don't come cheaply, so slowly build up your pantry. Add oils, grains, sweeteners and superfoods as you use them. No need to buy everything at once. Once purchased, a little does seem to go a long way. A good jar of raw honey can last months. Buying in bulk is another money-saving option. And save even the smallest amounts of ingredients. You never know, you may just need a teaspoon of almond flour tomorrow.

HEALTHY FATS AND OILS

I've learned *not* to shy away from fats. It took a while, though. Growing up in times of low-fat everything, I believed that fats were nothing but harmful. However, not only do fats give flavor and rich texture to foods, many can actually be beneficial to your health. Your body craves fats, and when you feed it the right ones in moderation, you'll feel full and satisfied. Fats also aid your body in absorbing fat-soluble vitamins.

I'd buy cold-pressed extra-virgin coconut oil by the truckload if I could. It has been shown that this fat, once thought of as very unhealthy, acts as an antibacterial agent, raises the body's metabolism, and is rich in medium-chain fatty acids, which increase the good HDL cholesterol level in the blood. It does have a slight flavor, but being the coconut lover I am, I find it enhances most dishes.

Coconut oil becomes liquid at 76°F, so it may liquefy in your cupboard on a hot day—but don't worry, it'll solidify again when it cools down, with no ill effects to the oil.

If you're not a fan of coconut flavor, consider aroma-free coconut oil, which has no taste and is a particularly good oil for frying. I like Omega Nutrition and Nutiva brands.

Because of its high smoking point, peanut oil, which contains valuable amounts of vitamin E, also works well for frying.

Extra-virgin olive oil, shown to lower total cholesterol, is my other can't-live-without fat. I even use it for popcorn (coconut oil works wonders with popcorn, too!).

Organic canola or grapeseed oils are what I use when I need a completely neutral oil.

Avocados, which are high in fiber and potassium, are another healthy monounsaturated fat I use often.

VINEGARS

Balsamic, apple cider, white wine, red wine, and rice wine are the basic vinegars I always keep in stock.

MILKS

For those who want to steer clear of dairy, the blender makes it easy. Homemade nut milks can be made in minutes. Almond and coconut milk are my favorites. If you purchase nondairy milks at the store, look for those with the fewest ingredients possible. And try to avoid coconut milk in the carton. Instead buy BPA-free canned coconut milk whenever possible.

Although it's not a milk, I like to use coconut water as a nondairy liquid in smoothies.

I don't avoid cow's milk myself (I was born in the dairy state of Wisconsin, after all), but I do use it sparingly. I just make sure it's always organic. I often use tangy buttermilk because it lends a rich flavor to baked goods. It also contains probiotic microbes, which makes it easier to digest than plain cow's milk.

NUTS AND SEEDS

The blender makes it a cinch to add nuts and seeds—which are packed with protein, nutrients, and healthy fats like omega-3s—to your diet. They both contain a high fat content though, which means they go rancid quickly. I store large amounts in the freezer and keep smaller portions in the pantry in airtight lidded glass jars.

I keep a wide array of nuts on hand including almonds, pecans, walnuts, pistachios, hazelnuts, cashews, and pine nuts.

buy both in bulk as it tends to be much less expensive.

My pantry is always chock-full of seeds, which I consider nutritional powerhouses. I like them for the crunch and nutty flavor they give to food. It's easy to add a handful to a smoothie or salad dressing. Sprinkle them over vegetables and main courses, too. I most often use flaxseeds, pumpkin seeds, chia seeds, and hemp seeds.

GRAINS, FLOURS, AND LEGUMES

Having a pantry loaded with a variety of grains and beans makes life so much easier, especially when you need to whip up a meal in minutes. You can turn to the cupboard and say, "Aha, I'll make *fill-in-the-blank* because I have *fill-in-the blank*."

Some of the basics that are good to have on hand include brown rice, old-fashioned rolled oats, quinoa, chickpeas, lentils, black beans, and peanuts.

I'm partial to dried beans for their texture and flavor, but canned beans work when you're pressed for time.

One of the best things you can make in a blender: fresh flours. Whole grains keep longer than ready-made flours, and making nut flours is so much more cost-effective than buying them.

SWEETENERS

I prefer things much less sweet today than I did even a year ago. I find that as I reduce my sugar intake, my taste buds adapt to my new eating habits. I continually try to use as little sugar as possible.

Although sugar is sugar is sugar and the goal is to reduce overall intake, when I do use sweetener, I tend to gravitate toward something less processed than standard white granulated sugar.

Raw honey is my sweetener of choice. There are many claims that it has curative properties, and while I can't confirm them, I do like that raw honey is unprocessed and unpasteurized, which means the goodness of honey is not destroyed by heat.

Maple syrup is another good sweetener. It contains some minerals and is especially high in manganese. I buy it from a local source who taps trees in our area.

There are some recipes that just work best with plain old sugar. In that case, I use unbleached organic cane sugar because at least I know it's grown without pesticides and is better for the earth. It's also said to be less processed than regular sugar.

HERBS AND SPICES

Small bowls with Diamond Crystal kosher salt and Maldon sea salt reside next to my stove at all times. Next to them stands a black pepper grinder. I probably use the contents of these three vessels more than anything else in my kitchen. I add a pinch of salt and twist of freshly ground pepper (don't use the type that comes preground) to almost everything.

When I don't have fresh herbs growing, I always make sure I have bunches of cilantro, parsley, rosemary, thyme, and tarragon on hand. I have an extensive dried spice drawer, but some essentials include cumin, coriander, ginger, cinnamon, and paprika.

Dijon mustard is another must-have. Creamy and sharp, it just gives that extra oomph to many vinaigrettes and sauces. I especially like Maille brand.

Tips and Tricks

LIQUIDS AND SOFT FOODS FIRST

How you load your blender may make a difference in your outcome, and keep things blending smoothly without extra spatula action. Add liquids and soft foods to the blender container first, then put the harder ingredients on top, including ice.

GO SLOWLY AND DON'T OVERPROCESS

I said it before and I'll say it again: *Do not* overblend. The blender is a powerful machine, and the consistency of something can go from great to ghastly in seconds. Just go slowly. Less is more. When your machine is whirring with nothing moving inside, stop it and push the ingredients toward the blade with a spatula. I rarely expect that everything will blend up evenly without a little help from a spatula. It's good to make sure all the bits of what you're blending are out from under the blades and fully integrated.

Also go easy on your machine. When it gets overly warm or starts to sputter, turn it off and let it cool down.

NO NEED TO MINCE

A primary advantage to using a blender is ease. I purposefully call for large pieces of vegetables and cloves of garlic only cut in half once to avoid lots of time spent dicing and chopping. Let the blender do the work. There may be one or two recipes where you do have to mince, but only because, for example, only half the soup gets blended in order to retain texture; in this case the garlic should be minced since not all of it will be pureed.

EVERYTHING TO TASTE

Almost every recipe in this book calls for salt, pepper, or some other type of seasoning. Use the amounts listed as a guide, but don't hesitate to use more or less according to your preference. Another beauty of blending is that unlike baking, it's not an exact science (that is, unless you're making something like blender brownies or a cake).

You can always add another squeeze of lime or sprig of cilantro and keep testing until the flavors seem balanced to you. If something tastes too sweet, add an acid; too sour, add a sweetener. Play around. Taste as you go.

EASY CLEANUP

The very best to way to clean your blender is to do it right away. Don't let food dry and harden inside the container. It only takes seconds to clean. Fill your blender about one-third full with hot water and a few drops of liquid dish soap. Place the lid on the blender, place the pitcher back on the base, and run it on low for a few seconds, then turn it to high for a minute. Pour out the water, rinse the blender with more hot water, and use a dish brush to scrub out any remaining food should there be any. That's it, your blender is clean!

SOAKING NUTS, SEEDS, GRAINS, AND LEGUMES

Lots of nuts, seeds, grains, and legumes are used in this book, and they all naturally contain phytic acid. Phytic acid binds to minerals and prevents them from being absorbed by our bodies. It's debatable whether phytates (phytic acid) should be of concern. However, to avoid them, you can soak nuts, seeds, grains, and legumes. Not only does soaking reduce phytic acid, it also neutralizes enzyme inhibitors that are present, which some say can cause trouble with digestion.

On a more functional level, soaking nuts makes them much easier to grind for nut milks. If you soak nuts before making nut butters, they must be thoroughly dried at a temperature below 150°F. Most ovens don't go that low (my lowest setting is 200°F), so keep the oven door slightly ajar and use an oven thermometer to regulate the temperature. It's said that if you heat the nuts above 150°F, you'll destroy the good enzymes. If you're really dedicated to soaking, consider purchasing a food dehydrator.

If this all seems like a lot of hassle, you can dry your nuts in an oven set to 300 to 350°F with the same taste result—or you can just blend them into a butter without soaking at all. Unless you're a strict vegetarian or your diet is restricted in other ways, you're likely to get the nutrients you need from other foods and still reap the other positive benefits of nuts and seeds without soaking them.

Tools

SPATULA
A good strong, dishwasher-safe silicone spatula with some bend and flexibility may be the single most important tool you'll want when working with the blender. It will help scrape all the good bits out, and will also help push ingredients toward the blade. I have several different sizes, including a small one for scraping under the blade.

SHARP PARING KNIFE AND CHEF'S KNIFE
While the blender blades will do most of your cutting and chopping, it's still good to have sharp knives on hand to cut up large fruits like watermelon and do more tedious jobs like removing ribs from kale. Always hand wash your knives and dry them immediately after each use.

FINE-MESH STRAINER/SIEVE
You'll find this simple kitchen tool indispensable for juices and straining purees and sauces.

NUT BAGS
Although you can use cheesecloth or a sieve, I find that a sturdy nylon drawstring bag works best when straining nut and seed milks.

ICE CUBE TRAYS
Pour leftover smoothies and purees into ice cube trays to make frozen cubes, which are easy to store and blend up again quite well.

RESEALABLE FREEZER BAGS
Good to have on hand for freezing fruit and other blender leftovers.

STORAGE CONTAINERS
French-made Luminarc glasses with airtight plastic storage lids are perfect for storing soups, juices, and more. They fit well in the fridge, and I like that they double as drinking glasses.

METAL STRAWS
Many years ago, I had a colleague who looked at me disapprovingly every time I used a plastic straw. "Do you know how unnecessary that is?" she would say to me. And she was right. I don't think I saw one straw when I was traveling in France recently. The French seem to consume their beverages just fine without them.

According to ecocycle.org, we use over 500 million straws in the United States each day. There are a plethora of reasons why we shouldn't use disposable plastic straws, including growing landfills, so I try to use metal and biodegradable paper ones whenever possible.

CAST-IRON PAN
This may seem like an odd essential for blender cooking, but a well-seasoned cast-iron skillet will fry up a blender burger with a restaurant-quality crispy crust. Its nonstick surface is also great for pancakes, and you can even bake brownies in it. They're inexpensive and can take the place of four pans. If I were stuck on a desert island and could have one kitchen tool, this would be it (unless, of course, I could get a solar-powered blender!).

CHAPTER 2

Nut Milks and Flours

It's astonishing how easy it is to make your own flours. When I think of the time I once once spent looking for almond flour, I'm regretful that I didn't know to just make it. Well, that will never happen again. With the aid of my blender, I can have freshly ground flours in minutes. Vitamins and minerals deteriorate quickly once grains are ground, so when you make your own flours, you reap Mother Nature's goodness packed into seed grains instead of it perishing on store shelves. Specialty flours like rice and coconut can also be pricey and hard to find. Grinding your own makes gluten-free options easily accessible at a fraction of retail cost.

The same goes for nut milks—when you make them yourself you're guaranteed a fresh product with zero preservatives at a budget-friendly price tag. You also greatly expand your options for dairy-free alternatives to cow's milk. There may be many types of almond milk available these days, but what about hemp seed milk? It's highly nutritious but may not be so easy to find. With the blender, it's yours for the making. And don't reserve these milks just for smoothies: Use them for savory sauces and sweets baking, too.

Almond Milk

An excellent alternative to dairy milk, silky-smooth almond milk is low in carbs, cholesterol- and lactose-free, easy to digest, and a good source of vitamin E.

1 cup almonds, soaked for 8 hours, then drained with water discarded

3 cups springwater or filtered tap water

Sweetener to taste, if desired

Place the nuts and water in the blender jar and process on high until combined and completely smooth. Add sweetener if desired.

Strain the mixture using a nut bag or strainer. Discard the pulp.

Chill and serve.

Brown Rice Milk

For those with a lactose or nut intolerance, brown rice milk is a good cow's or nut milk substitute because it's unlikely to trigger allergic reactions. Rice milk, which has a light, refreshing flavor, is low in fat but high in carbs.

¾ cup cooked brown rice

3 cups springwater or filtered tap water

Pinch of kosher salt

¼ teaspoon pure vanilla extract

Honey to taste, if desired

Place all the ingredients in the blender jar and process on high until combined and completely smooth. Discard the pulp.

Strain the mixture using a nut bag or strainer.

Chill and serve.

Hemp Seed Milk

makes about 4 cups

Considered a superfood, hemp seeds are one of the densest sources of plant proteins available. These power-packed kernels deliver protein and omega-3 essential fatty acids, which are essential to brain, skin, joint, and heart health. You can sprinkle them raw on almost anything, and when you blend the seeds into a milk, they give the beverage an especially creamy consistency.

1 cup shelled organic hemp seeds (also called hemp hearts)

3 cups springwater or filtered tap water

1 teaspoon raw honey

Place all the ingredients in the blender jar and process on high until combined and completely smooth.

Strain the mixture using a nut bag or strainer. Discard the pulp.

Chill and serve.

Coconut Milk

makes about 4 ½ cups

Rich with its creamy goodness and slight hint of coconut, this milk makes a delicious base for smoothies. Use it in cupcakes and muffins too.

2 cups unsweetened coconut or coconut flakes

4 cups springwater or filtered tap water

Soak the coconut in the water for 2 hours.

Place the coconut and the water in the blender jar and process on high for 2 minutes or until smooth.

Strain the coconut through a nut bag, squeezing out all the milk into a bowl. When you've squeezed out all you can, transfer the milk to a storage container and reserve the pulp to make coconut flour (page 35).

Chill and serve.

Coconut Flour

makes about 1 cup

My first adventures with coconut flour were not successful. Several years back I saw it on the store shelf and thought, Hmmm, let me see what I can make with this. *Well, I made a brick. Little did I know coconut flour is nowhere near a one-to-one substitute for grain-based flours. You may notice that many of the baked goods recipes calling for it contain a large number of eggs. This is because the flour is extremely absorbent; the eggs also help give structure to baked goods due to the lack of gluten. The flour, made from dried coconut milk pulp, is high in fiber and makes a good gluten-free option. Try Raspberry Swirl Cupcakes (page 212) for a gluten-free dessert made with coconut flour.*

About 1¼ cups pulp from 1 Coconut Milk recipe (page 32)

Preheat the oven to 200°F. Line a baking sheet with parchment paper. Spread the coconut pulp out in a thin layer, breaking up any clumps.

Place the sheet in the oven and bake for approximately 45 minutes, or until the pulp is completely dry.

Put the dried pulp in the blender and process on high for 1 to 2 minutes or until finely ground.

Store in an airtight container.

Almond Flour

I heart almond flour. From a sweet, meringue-based French macaron to Two-Bite Raspberry Financiers (page 73), this flour adds a subtle nutty flavor to foods. You may find that some recipes call for almond meal instead of almond flour. The only difference: Meal is made from whole or unblanched almonds, while flour is made from blanched almonds and is sometimes more finely ground.

Be cautious when making this flour: An extra second or two and your flour can turn to butter!

2 cups blanched almonds

Put the almonds in the blender jar and start on low, then turn to high for 30 to 60 seconds or until the almonds are finely ground into a powder.

White and Traditional Whole Wheat Flours

makes about 3 cups

White *whole wheat flour is the same as whole wheat flour in the sense that it's ground from the* entire *wheat kernel—unlike all-purpose white flour, which is bleached and the bran and germ removed. The difference is that* white *whole wheat flour is ground from a hard white wheat berry instead of a red wheat berry, like traditional whole wheat flour.*

The result: a flour that has all the nutritional advantages of traditional whole wheat but with a lighter color and milder taste.

Use it in cookies, pancakes, muffins, and other baked goods that don't require a fine white flour (the way angel food cake does, say, or delicate biscuits).

Grinding flour is so easy, there's almost no excuse not to do it, except perhaps you don't have the wheat berries. Well, you're in luck. Both King Arthur Flour and Bob's Red Mill sell red (if you want to make traditional whole wheat flour) and hard white wheat berries by the pound online.

Whole wheat flours are particularly difficult to store because they contain healthy but perishable oils. To keep the flour from going rancid, I like to grind my own in small quantities.

2 cups hard white wheat berries for white whole wheat flour or 2 cups red wheat berries (for traditional whole wheat flour)

Place the wheat berries in the blender jar and process on high for 1 minute or until the berries are finely ground into a powder.

Oat Flour

Oat flour is an excellent option for gluten-free baking. There are several recipes in this book—Herbed Goat Cheese Turkey Burgers (page 153) and Fudgy Gluten-Free Brownies (page 209) among others—that use it. Try oat flour in muffins and quick breads, too.

1 cup organic old-fashioned rolled oats

Place the oats in the blender jar and start on low, then turn to high for 30 to 60 seconds, stopping once or twice to push the mixture toward the blade with a spatula, or until the oats are finely ground into a powder.

Store in an airtight container.

Chickpea Flour

Often used in Middle Eastern cooking, this gluten-free flour, also called garbanzo bean flour, has a slightly stronger flavor than other non-wheat flours. Try it in savory pancake or fritter recipes.

1 cup dried chickpeas

Place the chickpeas in the blender jar (a grain container if you have one) and process on high for 30 to 60 seconds or until the beans are finely ground.

Push the mixture through a fine-mesh sieve or a flour sifter. Put the larger pieces left in the sieve back into the blender and process again for at least another minute. Repeat the process until you have a fine, smooth flour.

Store in an airtight container.

Quinoa Flour

Quinoa flour is my all-time favorite gluten-free flour, in part because of the goodness it delivers—high fiber and essential amino acids—but I'm also particularly fond of its earthy flavor. You can simply grind quinoa grains to make flour, so if you're in a rush, don't hesitate to do so. A few minutes of toasting though mellows the flavor and makes a finer flour when ground.

1¾ cups quinoa

Preheat the oven to 350 degrees. Spread the quinoa in a single layer on a large baking sheet. Use two sheets if necessary. Toast the quinoa in the oven for about 15 minutes. Do not let it brown.

Remove the quinoa from the oven and allow it to cool. Place it in the blender jar and start on low then turn to high for 30 to 60 seconds or until the grains are finely ground into a powder. Store in an airtight container.

White Rice Flour

makes about 2¼ cups

Light and silken, this flour is superb for coating chicken, eggplant, and other oven-fried foods. It's also a popular substitute for all-purpose flour in many gluten-free baked goods. You can make brown rice flour as easily by substituting dry brown rice for the white. Brown rice flour makes an excellent binder in meatless burgers.

2 cups dry white rice | Put the rice in the blender jar and start on low, then turn to high for 30 to 60 seconds or until the rice is finely ground into the desired consistency.

White Cornmeal

makes about 1½ cups

The connection between popcorn and cornmeal was one I had not made prior to owning a blender. Yes, of course I knew they were both derived from corn—but popcorn is what you eat at the movies and I use cornmeal for, among other things, breads and dusting pizza crusts. But I was not thinking the obvious: Popcorn kernels are dried corn. Cornmeal is ground dried corn kernels. Popcorn in the blender = cornmeal. Voilà!

1 cup unpopped white popcorn kernels | Put the popcorn in the blender jar (a grain container if you have one) and process on low for 5 seconds. Turn the power to high and blend for another 30 seconds or until very fine.

CHAPTER 3

Healthy Drinks

So what's better, juicing or blending? Hmmm, hard to say. They each have their place. To juice is to extract the liquid from fruits or vegetables and remove the pulp. Blending pulverizes the produce to make a smooth drink. The biggest difference: Smoothies can be loaded with fiber while juices naturally can't. However, both can be nutrient-packed. Personally, I drink smoothies more often, but I still can't resist a cool, revitalizing glass of juice. Either way, filling your blender with locally grown greens, freshly picked berries, and homemade nut milks can only be a good thing.

Blender drinks are an excellent way to add the USDA-recommended five daily servings of fruits and vegetables to your diet. So use the following recipes as guidelines, but don't hesitate to voyage out on your own. Be creative. Experiment with your own favorite combinations and change up your ingredients according to what's in season. It'll help ensure that every sip is delicious, and variety provides a broad range of nutrients.

Flash freezing fruits and vegetables at their peak of freshness helps preserve vitamins, and will expand your options to a rainbow of choices during those lackluster, produce-poor winter months. These quick and easy drinks are a super-healthy way to start the day, or sometimes even end it. Cheers.

Cool Mint Slush

Refreshing and smooth, this icy concoction will cool you down on the hottest of days. A splash of vodka or gin turns this drink into a delightful summer cocktail. Whip up a batch in advance and freeze in a resealable plastic bag. When you're ready to use it, break up the mixture in the sealed bag then add it to the blender container, pulse several times, and serve.

1 whole lemon, cut into quarters, seeds removed

¾ cup freshly squeezed lemon juice (juice of about 3 lemons)

⅓ cup raw honey, or more to taste

¼ cup water

4 cups ice

½ cup fresh mint leaves, plus extra for garnish

Add the cut lemon and lemon juice to the container and blend on medium-high until smooth.

Add the honey, water, and ice and continue to blend until completely smooth.

Put the mint in the container and pulse five or six times, until the mint is chopped and mixed through-out. Serve garnished with mint leaves.

Mango and Greek Yogurt Freeze

This drink delivers the essence of mangoes, which are at their best in spring and summer. Mangoes that are green and hard should ripen after a few days at room temperature. The feel and smell of the mango are much more important than the color. Never refrigerate unripe mangoes. If ripe mangoes aren't available, look for jarred mango in the produce section or bags of mango chunks in the frozen food section, now available from Trader Joe's and Dole. When mangoes are in season (and usually on sale), I buy them in bulk, cut the fruit into chunks, and freeze it in airtight containers.

1 cup fresh mango chunks
½ cup plain Greek yogurt
1 cup ice
1 teaspoon raw honey or other sweetener to taste

Place all the ingredients in the blender pitcher in the order listed. Blend for 20 seconds on low then turn to high for another 40 to 60 seconds or until the mixture is completely smooth.

AM Energy Booster

There's no doubt that this thick, shake-like smoothie will never win a beauty contest. Its brownish-bluish tint does not have the seductive power of a ravishing red raspberry smoothie, nor does it taste like a dessert beverage. However, this drink is a powerhouse. I consume some form of this less-than-sexy concoction at least three out of seven mornings—I substitute hemp milk, add pumpkin seeds, change up the fruit and greens. It's like an elixir. It keeps me moving straight ahead, with no horrible highs or lows. The almond butter, which is a predominant flavor in this smoothie, helps regulate blood sugar, and the fiber-rich chia and hemp seeds add essential amino acids and omega-3 fats that keep me full and happy until lunch.

1½ cups coconut water

1 tablespoon freshly squeezed lemon juice

1 cup loosely packed baby kale, spinach, or other greens

1 cup frozen cherries

½ cup frozen blueberries

2 tablespoons almond butter

2 tablespoons chia seeds

1 tablespoon hemp seeds

½–1 cup ice

Place all the ingredients in the blender pitcher in the order listed. Blend for 20 seconds on low, then turn to high for another 40 to 60 seconds or until the mixture is completely smooth. Add more water if you find the consistency too thick and blend again. Drink immediately.

Pure Strawberry Banana Smoothie

serves 2

Strawberries and bananas are enhanced by the sweet, earthy flavor of hemp milk, an extremely beneficial non-dairy milk alternative that is a breeze to make (page 32). It's hard to believe this creamy, dessert-like drink, with 10 essential amino acids, is actually good for you!

2 cups hemp milk

2 frozen bananas, peeled and cut into large chunks

1 pint (2 cups) frozen strawberries, hulled

Place all the ingredients in the blender pitcher in the order listed above. Blend for 20 seconds on low, then turn to high for another 40 to 60 seconds or until the mixture is completely smooth.

from left to right: Coconut Almond Smoothie, Cranberry Orange Frappe, Pure Strawberry Banana Smoothie, Revitalizing Raw Green Juice

Revitalizing Raw Green Juice

serves 2

Go green! A mix of fruits and veggies gives this drink an agreeable balance between sweet and bitter. Don't hesitate to mix up your greens here—kale, spinach, beet greens—for a variety of tastes. You can drink this as a smoothie, too; just skip the straining and add 1 cup ice when blending.

1 cup unsweetened iced green tea

½ apple, peeled, cored, and cut into quarters

2 Swiss chard leaves, stem removed

1 romaine leaf

¼ cucumber, seeded and cut into quarters

1 tablespoon freshly squeezed lemon juice

¼ cup flat-leaf parsley leaves

1-inch piece gingerroot, peeled

15 green grapes

Place all the ingredients in the blender pitcher in the order listed above. Blend for 10 seconds on medium, then turn to high for 1 more minute.

Push the mixture through a fine-mesh strainer. Chill to serve or pour over ice.

Beet and Carrot Juice Tonic

serves 1

Boost your stamina and immunity with this vitamin-loaded juice. The combination of carrots and beets does tend to become thick, though, so don't hesitate adding more water to obtain a thinner consistency. Pouring it over a full glass of ice will also help dilute this juice.

¼–½ cup coconut water or springwater, depending on desired consistency

1 medium orange, peeled and divided into sections

2 medium carrots, washed and cut into 2-inch chunks

3 beets (about 5-7 ounces total), washed and quartered

Place everything in the blender pitcher in the order listed. Blend on low for 30 seconds, turn the dial to medium and blend for 15 seconds more, then turn to high and blend for 1 minute.

Push the mixture through a fine-mesh strainer. Blend a second time for an even smoother consistency. Chill to serve or pour over ice.

Cranberry Orange Frappe

serves 2

Fresh. Bright. Zingy. This vitamin C booster will wake up your taste buds with its citrusy tang. Not just for breakfast, this drink makes a stimulating afternoon snack.

½ cup almond milk

1 cup frozen cranberries

1 whole orange, peeled and broken into segments

¼ teaspoon ground cinnamon

1–2 teaspoons maple syrup, or more to taste

1 cup ice

Place all the ingredients in the blender pitcher in the order listed. Blend for 20 seconds on low, then turn to high for another 40 to 60 seconds or until the mixture is completely smooth.

Pumpkin Spice Smoothie

serves 2

Like the smell of burning leaves or apple cider dough-nuts, this smoothie will transport you to a place of autumnal happiness. Sip this creamy concoction through a straw and you'll swear you're slurping up a pumpkin pie.

1 cup canned pumpkin
1 cup coconut milk
1 cup ice
1 small frozen banana, cut into several pieces
1 tablespoon maple syrup
½ teaspoon ground cinnamon
¼ teaspoon ground nutmeg
¼ teaspoon ground ginger
⅛ teaspoon ground cloves
¼ teaspoon orange zest

Place all the ingredients in the blender pitcher in the order listed. Blend for 5 seconds on low, then turn to high for another 20 seconds or until the mixture is completely smooth.

Coconut Almond Smoothie

serves 1

Smooth and creamy, this milky drink has a pleasing nutty flavor. Using homemade coconut milk adds an even richer taste. It's kind of like an Almond Joy with-out the chocolate. If you want it to mimic the candy bar even more, shave a little dark chocolate on top.

1 cup coconut milk
1 tablespoon almond butter
5 dates, pitted
1 teaspoon pure vanilla extract (optional)
1½ cups ice

Place all the ingredients in the blender pitcher in the order listed. Blend for 20 seconds on low, then turn to high for another 40 to 60 seconds or until the mixture is completely smooth.

Refreshing Pineapple Ginger Juice

serves 4

I learned to make this downright addictive drink from a bartender at The Rockhouse in Negril, Jamaica. After seeing it listed on the breakfast menu under juices simply as "Homemade," my family and I were intrigued. One morning we took the plunge and ordered it. We never looked back. When I asked the waitress about the fresh and spicy drink, she told me the bartenders made it. The very friendly Naason showed me how. He blended up the whole pineapple, peel and all, in his Vitamix. It takes a little time, but it is worth every second of effort. It's also inviting as an afternoon cocktail with a little Jamaican rum.

1 whole pineapple, cored and cut into chunks

⅓ cup (2 ounces) fresh unpeeled gingerroot, chopped into pieces

2 cups springwater or filtered tap water

Raw honey to taste

Place the pineapple, ginger, and water in a blender and process on medium-high until the mixture is fully blended (as smooth as you can get it).

Place a fine-mesh strainer over a bowl or container and pour in the pineapple-ginger mixture. Using the back of a spoon, press the mixture against the strainer, extracting as much of the juice as possible. You could use a nut bag, too.

Put the pineapple mash in the strainer back into the blender and process again on high. Strain again to extract more liquid from the mixture.

After your second strain, you should have about 36 ounces. If not, you may want to blend and strain the mixture one more time.

Finally, add honey to taste and stir to combine. Chill and serve over ice.

Watermelon Cucumber
Agua Fresca

makes **2 quarts**

Agua fresca *or "fresh water" is simply water infused with the essence of fruit. The thirst-quenching drink has just a hint of flavor. It's not too sweet, and is best when made with seasonally fresh fruit (experiment with different combinations including melons, pineapple, and mango). Serve it icy cold.*

4 cups springwater or filtered tap water

½ large watermelon, cut into large chunks (about 8 generous cups)

1 cucumber (about 2 cups)

¼ cup raw honey or to taste

6 basil leaves, for garnish

Put half the water, watermelon, and cucumber in the blender and run on low for 5 seconds. Then turn to high and process for 25 seconds or until pureed. Push the mixture through a fine-mesh strainer into a 2-quart pitcher.

Repeat the process with the rest of the ingredients, adding the honey this time. Pour the second strained mixture into the first. Stir and chill. Serve over ice and garnish with basil leaves.

CHAPTER 4

Breakfasts

While a smoothie makes a mighty nice meal replacement, it just doesn't give the same comforting feel as a big, hearty breakfast.
Mind you, a generous meal need not equal sugary, butter-laden dishes. With a few tweaks here and there, white-flour waffles are made gluten-free with a buckwheat substitution, pancakes are powered with chia seeds, and breakfast bread is loaded with fruits and veggies for a low-sugar, high-fiber treat.

Weekend breakfasts are my all-time favorite. Whether it's just the family or we have guests, we always make it extra special with table linens, a small vase of flowers or pine sprigs in winter, and even a candle or two. All these recipes work well for a crowd. Waffles and crêpes can be made before the meal and kept warm in a low oven; toppings like coulis and tarragon sauce can be made in advance. These are meals when you'll want smoothies as a supplement.

Buckwheat Waffles with Two-Berry Coulis

makes about 15 7-inch waffles

Do you know that buckwheat has nothing to do with wheat? It's not even a grain. It's a flowering herb whose starchy seeds are harvested and are available in many forms, from hulled, whole raw kernels to ground flours; toasted buckwheat kernels are often referred to as kasha. Buckwheat, which is closely related to rhubarb and sorrel, is gluten-free and ranks low on the glycemic scale. I've experimented with the flour quite a bit recently as my brother-in-law is diabetic and has celiac disease. In this recipe I use light buckwheat flour because it gives a lighter texture to the waffles. I am partial to Bouchard Family Farms Acadian Light Buckwheat Flour. If you can't find it and use dark buckwheat flour (which is visibly darker in appearance), use 1 cup white whole wheat flour in place of 1 cup buckwheat flour for these waffles. Buckwheat flour makes a great fried chicken coating too. Fried chicken and waffles anyone?

3 large eggs

2 cups buttermilk

1 teaspoon pure vanilla extract

1¾ cups light buckwheat flour

¼ cup organic cane sugar

¼ teaspoon kosher salt

1 tablespoon baking powder

½ cup aroma-free coconut oil, melted or canola oil

Fresh blackberries, red raspberries, and strawberries

Two-Berry Coulis (recipe follows)

Put the eggs, buttermilk, and vanilla in the blender. Process on medium for 15 seconds.

Next, add the flour, sugar, salt, and baking powder. Pulse several more times until the ingredients are just combined.

Lastly, add the oil and pulse until mixed together.

Bake in a preheated waffle iron on a medium setting. Make sure the waffles bake until they're somewhat crispy. Serve with fresh berries and Two-Berry Coulis.

Two-Berry Coulis

1 pint (2 cups) red raspberries

1 pint (2 cups) strawberries

¼ cup water

3 tablespoons organic cane sugar, or to taste, depending on the sweetness of the berries

Put the berries, water, and 3 tablespoons sugar in a small saucepan. Cook over medium heat, stirring constantly, for about 10 minutes.

Next, pour the mixture in the blender and run for 10 seconds on high. Pour the mixture through a fine-mesh strainer back into the saucepan. Use the back of a spoon to push as much of the sauce through the sieve as possible and bring it to a gentle boil for 3 minutes. Allow to cool. Serve over Buckwheat Waffles.

Crêpes

- 4 eggs
- 2 cups milk
- a splash of vanilla extract
- 1/2 tsp salt
- 2 cups flour
- 4 tbsp melted butter

Sweet Spelt Flour Crêpes

makes about 14 crêpes

This recipe belongs to my 12-year-old daughter, who has been making crêpes since she was 9. A self-taught crêpe maker, Camilla combed cookbooks for instruction, and then has perfected her skill over the years (all three of them!). She got a few pointers from a good friend of ours who lives in Montréal, and another book tipped her off to the magic of the blender—using it whips up crêpe batter to the perfect consistency.

When in France recently we noticed that many savory crêpes were made with buckwheat, which led us to experiment with different flours. I've made my own adjustment to Camilla's recipe and substituted spelt flour for the white flour she uses. It gives a faint nutty flavor to the thin pancakes, which are so delectable they barely need a filling. A squeeze of lemon and sprinkle of sugar is the perfect complement to the delicate pancake, although a few strawberries and hazelnut spread are pretty darn good on them, too.

4 large eggs
2 cups milk
½ teaspoon pure vanilla extract
2 cups spelt flour
½ teaspoon kosher salt
¼ cup melted unsalted butter, plus more for greasing the pan

Put the eggs, milk, and vanilla in the blender and process on medium for 15 seconds. Add the flour and salt and pulse several times. Add the butter and mix for 10 more seconds.

Melt about 2 teaspoons butter over medium heat in a nonstick 12-inch skillet. Spread the butter evenly around.

Pour 2 to 3 tablespoons of batter in the pan. Cook for 1 minute then flip the crêpe over and cook for another minute. The thinner the batter, the better. Continue to cook crêpes until all the batter is used.

Sweet Spelt Flour Crêpes shown with Quick Strawberry Spread (front) and Cardamom Peach Spread , and Dark Chocolate Hazelnut Spread (rear)

Chia Seed Pancakes

makes about twenty
4-inch pancakes

Chia seeds, which can be eaten whole, don't need to be ground to access their great health benefits. Tiny black and white chia seeds are a great source of protein and calcium and will boost the fiber content of your pancakes while giving them the slightest crunchy texture. Sounds strange for a pancake, I know, but it really adds an interesting new dimension to an old favorite.

2 cups buttermilk

1 large egg

1 teaspoon pure vanilla extract

1 tablespoon organic cane sugar

1½ cups white whole wheat flour

1 tablespoon baking powder

2 tablespoons chia seeds

1–2 tablespoons coconut oil or unsalted butter

Put the buttermilk, egg, and vanilla in the blender pitcher. Pulse on medium several times.

Next, add the sugar, flour, and baking powder to the pitcher and pulse again two or three times until just blended. Do not overmix; this will result in tough pancakes.

Add the chia seeds and pulse one more time.

Place a griddle or frying pan over medium heat. Add 1 tablespoon of the coconut oil or butter and use a spatula to spread it around the griddle or pan as it melts.

Transfer the batter from the blender pitcher to the griddle or skillet using a tablespoon measure, about 2 tablespoons per pancake. Spread the batter into a circle shape with the back of the spoon.

Cook until small bubbles appear and start to burst uniformly over the pancakes. Carefully flip the pancakes and cook for several more minutes on the other side. When golden brown on both sides, transfer to a serving platter. Continue to cook pancakes until all the batter is used, adding more oil or butter to the pan as needed.

Serve with warm maple syrup.

Two-Bite Raspberry Financiers

makes **24**

These little French-inspired cakes get their distinct flavor from beurre noisette *or brown butter. They are the perfect early-morning snack to have awaiting guests. Make the batter the night before, and within minutes the next morning, a sweet smell will be wafting through your house.*

½ cup (1 stick) unsalted butter, cut into 1-inch pieces, plus more for greasing the pans

¾ cup almond flour (page 36)

¼ cup all-purpose flour

⅔ cup confectioners' sugar

½ teaspoon baking powder

⅛ teaspoon kosher salt

5 large egg whites

1 teaspoon raw honey

½ teaspoon vanilla extract

½ pint (1 cup) red raspberries

Heat the butter in a small pan over medium-high heat, stirring it constantly. Keep stirring as the butter begins to bubble and foam. It will begin to brown in about 3 to 4 minutes (you'll see small bits on the bottom of the pan). When it does, remove it from the heat and set aside. Note that the butter goes from brown to burned very quickly.

Put the flours, sugar, baking powder, and salt in the blender and run for 10 seconds on high. Using a spatula, scrape the flours from the bottom of the mixer and run for another 10 seconds. Add the egg whites, honey, and vanilla; pulse three times. Do not overmix.

Transfer the batter to a bowl and stir in the browned butter. Cover with plastic wrap and refrigerate for at least 2 hours or up to 5 days.

Heat the oven to 400°F. Thoroughly butter a 24-cup mini muffin pan. Remove the batter from the refrigerator and stir. Fill each cup with a tablespoon of batter and top with one or two red raspberries.

Bake for 13 to 15 minutes or until the financiers are lightly browned and they spring back to the touch.

Spinach Egg Cups

Made in a cupcake pan, these egg cups could be likened to a crustless quiche. They're good on their own, but also make divine breakfast sandwiches placed between two slices of thick, buttered toast. Another option: Serve them on a bed of lightly dressed greens for a simple lunch.

1-inch piece shallot, skin removed

6 large eggs

½ cup milk

½ cup ricotta cheese

2 teaspoons all-purpose flour

¾ teaspoon kosher salt

⅛ teaspoon freshly-ground black pepper

½ teaspoon dried thyme

⅛ teaspoon freshly grated nutmeg

1½ cups baby spinach leaves

1 cup grated Gruyère cheese

Preheat the oven to 375°F. Grease a 12-cup muffin pan with cooking spray. Set aside. Place the shallot in the blender jar and pulse on medium a few times.

Add the eggs, milk, ricotta cheese, flour, salt, pepper, thyme, and nutmeg. Blend on medium for 5 seconds (do not overblend or the mixture will become too aerated).

Add the spinach to the blender and pulse two or three times, again being careful not overblend—or the mixture will turn green!

Stir in the grated cheese using a spoon or spatula.

Fill each muffin cup with ¼ cup egg mixture. Bake for 25 minutes or until slightly golden. Allow them to cool slightly before removing from the pan. Slide a sharp knife gently around the edges so you can slide them out easily.

Poached Eggs with Fried Tomatoes and Creamy Tarragon Sauce

serves **4–6**

The eggs and tomatoes here are really only a vehicle for the oh-so-good Creamy Tarragon Sauce. You could serve this sauce on a mud pie and it would probably make it edible. I like to add a side of arugula to this dish for a gluten-free vegetarian meal, but you could also add Canadian bacon and an English muffin to make it more like traditional eggs Benedict.

Creamy Tarragon Sauce (following)

1 large tomato, cut Into ¾-inch-thick slices

Kosher salt and freshly ground pepper to taste

1 tablespoon extra-virgin olive oil

2 tablespoons white vinegar

6 large eggs

Make the Creamy Tarragon Sauce and set aside.

Next, season each tomato slice on both sides with salt and pepper. Heat the olive oil in a skillet over medium-high heat. Fry the tomatoes for about 2 minutes on each side. Set aside.

Fill a medium-sized saucepan with water, bring it to high boil, then reduce to below simmering.

Add the vinegar to the water.

Crack one egg in a shallow cup or bowl and gently slide the egg into the water. Repeat with another egg. Cook two to three eggs at a time, until all the eggs are poached.

Using a slotted spoon, push the whites near their yolks so they don't settle on the bottom of the pan.

Let the eggs cook for 2 to 5 minutes (2 to 3 minutes for a runny yolk), then remove them gently with the spoon. Gently blot each egg with a paper towel and place it on top of a pan-fried tomato. Top each egg-tomato combo with a few spoonfuls of Creamy Tarragon Sauce. Season with salt and pepper and serve.

Creamy Tarragon Sauce

makes ¾ cup

3 large egg yolks

2 tablespoons freshly squeezed lemon juice

¼ teaspoon kosher salt

¾ cup (1½ sticks) unsalted butter, melted

1 tablespoon fresh tarragon or ½ teaspoon dried tarragon

Put the egg yolks, lemon juice, and salt in the blender and process on high for 30 seconds.

Pour the butter through the top of blender in a thin stream while it runs on medium for another 30 seconds or until thickened.

Add the tarragon and pulse one or two more times.

Zucchini Apple Muffins

I like to use white whole wheat flour in these muffins, which has the nutritional value of traditional whole wheat but with a milder flavor. You can grind your own (page 39), or use the white whole wheat from King Arthur brand—a superb product.

2 large eggs

⅓ cup canola oil or coconut oil, melted

¼ cup unsweetened applesauce

¾ cup dark brown sugar, firmly packed

1 tablespoon orange zest (from about 1 large orange)

1 tablespoon freshly squeezed orange juice

2 teaspoons pure vanilla extract

1 medium zucchini, cut in half lengthwise then into 2-inch chunks (about 2 heaping cups or 12 ounces)

1¼ cups spelt flour

1 cup white whole wheat flour

2 teaspoons baking powder

¼ teaspoon baking soda

1½ teaspoons ground cinnamon

¾ teaspoon ground ginger

¼ teaspoon ground cloves

½ teaspoon kosher salt

1 small apple, peeled and cut into ½-inch chunks (about 1 heaping cup)

Preheat the oven to 350°F. Line a muffin pan with paper liners.

Put the eggs, oil, applesauce, brown sugar, orange zest and juice, and vanilla extract in the blender in that order. Run on medium for 15 seconds or until just combined.

Add the zucchini and pulse three times.

In a large bowl, whisk together the flours, baking powder, baking soda, spices, and salt. Fold the mixture from the blender into the dry ingredients until just combined. Do not overmix. Stir in the apple chunks.

Fill each muffin cup with a ¼-cup measure. Bake for 15 minutes or until a toothpick comes out clean. Serve with Whipped Citrus Zest Butter (page 90).

Tempting Banana Coconut Loaf

makes 1 loaf

This rich, dense breakfast bread, loaded with bananas, pineapple, and coconut, conjures up an island feel. Oats and flaxseed also contribute to the goodness of this healthy—yet still sweet and moist—morning treat.

1½ cups white whole wheat flour

½ cup old-fashioned rolled oats

¼ cup ground flaxseed

2 teaspoons baking powder

½ teaspoon kosher salt

¾ cup shredded unsweetened coconut

2 large eggs

½ cup coconut oil, melted

¾ cup dark brown sugar

1 teaspoon pure vanilla extract

3 medium-sized ripe bananas, cut into chunks

1 8-ounce can crushed pineapple, very well drained (a heaping ½ cup)

Preheat the oven to 350°F. Grease a 9 x 5-inch loaf pan and line with parchment paper so it overhangs the sides by an inch.

In a large bowl, whisk together the flour, oats, flaxseed, baking powder, salt, and unsweetened coconut.

Next, place the eggs, coconut oil, brown sugar, and vanilla in the blender. Run on medium for 15 seconds.

Scrape down the sides of the blender, add the bananas and pineapple, and pulse three times.

Fold the mixture from the blender into the dry ingredients and until just combined.

Pour the batter into the prepared pan and bake for 50 minutes to 1 hour or until the top becomes a dark golden brown and a toothpick inserted into the center of the loaf comes out clean.

CHAPTER 5

Nut Butters and Fruit Spreads

Just like flours and dairy-free milks, nut butters are another pantry staple made easy with the blender. Because you know exactly what you're putting in the blender container, you know exactly what you're putting in your body. You control the types of nuts—raw, organic, roasted, soaked—the amount of sugar and what kind, the salt, and whatever else you decide to add.

Nut butters may have a high fat content, but it's good fat, fat that makes you feel full and satisfied, fat that keeps you from snacking all day on empty-calorie junk foods. Nut butters, which contain fiber, protein, and antioxidants, make excellent sandwich spreads, but they're also great additions to smoothies and sauces.

You can use the blender to enhance cow's milk butter with fruit zests and even whip up a quick fruit butter or spread. The possibilities here are numerous. Get creative with your blends. Combine a nut butter and coconut butter or several fruits into a spread.

Creamy Cashew Butter

For some reason, this extremely rich and ultra-creamy nut butter seems more decadent than others. And I suppose it is. With slightly less fiber and protein, cashew butter doesn't quite deliver the nutrition almond and peanut butters do. However, cashews still provide important minerals and amino acids, so it's not exactly a senseless indulgence, just relatively speaking. Try adding a tablespoon or two of cashew to sauces for added richness and depth.

2 cups raw cashews, soaked, or 2 cups roasted cashews

1 tablespoon aroma-free coconut oil, melted, plus more for rubbing the sides

¼ teaspoon kosher salt

If you're using roasted cashews, skip to the last step. If you're soaking your cashews, cover the raw nuts with water and soak for 3 hours.

After 3 hours, preheat the oven to 300°F. Drain and rinse the nuts, then spread them on a parchment-lined baking sheet in a single layer. Roast them in the oven for 20 to 30 minutes or until they are completely dry. If not, the nuts will not turn to butter. Toss the nuts with salt.

Rub the inside of the blender jar with melted coconut oil. Place the roasted nuts in the blender with the oil and run on low for approximately 10 minutes, or until smooth, stopping and scraping down the sides of the blender every 2 to 3 minutes.

Dark Chocolate Hazelnut Spread

makes about ¾ cup

Yes, you got it! Homemade you-know-what. Hazelnuts and cocoa powder. Yum. This variant is slightly nuttier than the Italian jarred brand, which lists sugar as the first ingredient. All the more reason to make it at home—you know exactly how much of what you're putting in that blender jar!

1½ cups whole hazelnuts

8 ounces bittersweet chocolate chips

2 tablespoons mild oil, such as aroma-free coconut or canola, plus more for rubbing the sides

2 tablespoons unsweetened cocoa powder

2 tablespoons confectioners' sugar

1 tablespoon pure vanilla extract

½ teaspoon kosher salt

Preheat the oven to 375°F. Spread the nuts in a single layer on a baking sheet and bake in the oven for about 10 minutes. Allow the nuts to cool for several minutes. Lay a dishtowel out on the counter and spread the hazelnuts out on it. Lay another dish towel on top and rub the nuts between the two towels to remove the skins.

Melt the chocolate in a double boiler and allow to cool.

Rub the inside of the blender jar generously with oil. Place the skinned, toasted nuts in the blender and process on low for 10 seconds. Increase to medium. Scrape down the sides and run on low for 2 minutes. Add the oil and run on low another 2 minutes. Scrape down the sides again and continue running until the nuts form a paste (about 8 minutes total). Add the rest of the ingredients except the melted chocolate and process for another minute or until creamy smooth.

Finally, add the melted chocolate and blend again until a spreadable consistency is reached. If the mixture became warm while processing in your blender, it will thicken up slightly as it cools.

Maple Pecan Butter

makes 1 cup

A friend of mine told me this melt-in-your-mouth butter reminded her of Thanksgiving. No reason to reserve this dessert-like nut butter for fall, though. The pecan-cinnamon-maple flavor combination is a delightful treat year-round.

2 cups pecans

1 tablespoon grapeseed oil or aroma-free coconut oil

1 tablespoon maple syrup

¼ teaspoon ground cinnamon

Heat a skillet over medium-high heat. Put in the pecans and toast them for 5 to 7 minutes, stirring frequently.

Next, put the toasted pecans in the blender and run on low for 2 minutes. Turn the power to medium and continue to blend until the nut mixture starts to become creamy. Stop and push the nuts toward the blender blades during the processing time if necessary. The process may take upward of 10 minutes but may happen in 3.

Last, add the oil, maple syrup, and cinnamon, and blend until smooth.

Sweet Pistachio Butter

You may wonder how something so greenish brown can taste so good. I just couldn't bear to leave this recipe out of the book based on its unattractive color, though. I feel I'd be cheating you of a delicious treat. If you want to achieve a vibrant pistachio-green butter, you can remove the purply-brown skins from the pistachios. It does take a long time, though, and the skins don't affect the taste, just the lovely color! Use pistachio butter as a replacement for peanut butter in cookie or bar recipes, or simply spread it on toast.

2 cups pistachios, shelled
1 tablespoon raw honey
½ teaspoon kosher salt

Preheat the oven to 375°F. Spread the nuts on a parchment-lined baking sheet in a single layer then roast for 5 to 7 minutes or until they become fragrant.

Place the pistachios in the blender with the honey and salt. Blend on low for 10 minutes, stopping and scraping down the sides of the blender every 2 to 3 minutes. This process takes patience and the time may vary greatly. Just continue blending and I assure it will turn to butter.

Smooth Almond Butter

makes 1¾ cups

I don't know if almond butter will ever replace peanut butter as an American staple, but if you can get past the nostalgia of a good ol' pb&j, you'll find almond butter has some benefits over peanut butter: higher iron and magnesium levels, more fiber, plus a good dose of vitamin E. And let's not forget how delicious it is!

3 cups raw almonds

2 tablespoons coconut oil, melted, plus more for rubbing the sides

Soak the almonds for 8 hours or overnight. Drain and rinse the nuts, then spread them on a parchment-lined baking sheet in a single layer. Bake them in the oven for 1½ hours at 300°F or until they are completely dry.

Rub the inside of the blender jar with melted coconut oil. Place the nuts in the blender with the oil and run on low for 10 seconds. Then turn the blender to high and run for approximately 2 more minutes until the nuts become smooth and creamy.

Rich Coconut Butter

makes 1 cup

Spread this tasty tropical treat on toast in place of cow's butter, or use a spoonful in smoothies or sauces. One tablespoon contains two grams of fiber!

4 cups unsweetened coconut flakes (12-ounce package such as Bob's Red Mill)

Place the coconut flakes in the blender and run for 30 seconds on medium speed. Using a spatula, scrape down the sides and bottom of the blender jar, pushing the coconut toward the blade.

Run the blender on high for 2½ minutes or until the mixture becomes smooth and creamy. Store in a jar at room temperature for up to three months (if you don't eat it sooner!).

Whipped Citrus Zest Butter

makes about 1 cup

With just a little zest and sweetener, you can transform butter into something unexpected. It's divine spread on Zucchini Apple Muffins (page 78). Try it on scones, too.

1 cup (2 sticks) unsalted butter, softened
1 tablespoon lemon zest
1 tablespoon orange zest
1 tablespoon freshly squeezed orange juice
1 tablespoon raw honey

Place all the ingredients in the blender jar and run for 5 to 10 seconds or until thoroughly mixed. Store in the refrigerator in an airtight container for up to one week.

Quick Strawberry Spread

When I was living in Norway, a friend said, "I'll make a quick jam for breakfast." How's she going to do that? *I thought. Within minutes she placed strawberry jam on the table. This sweet spread that epitomizes fresh berries is a version of her recipe. I'd like to call it jam but hesitate to do so because it is most likely* not *what you traditionally think of as jam. There is no canning or pectin involved, so it's a little runnier than classic American jam. The downside is that the spread will only last in the fridge for about a week. The upside: You can have it in minutes.*

1 quart strawberries, hulled

⅓ cup organic cane sugar

1 tablespoon freshly squeezed lemon juice

1 teaspoon lemon zest

Place all the ingredients in a medium saucepan and cook over medium-high heat for 10 minutes, stirring frequently.

Allow the mixture to cool for 5 minutes. Put it in the blender and pulse two or three times. Serve immediately.

Cardamom Peach Spread

makes 2¾ cups

Similar to the Quick Strawberry Spread, this peach spread is thinner than traditional preserves. Spoon it over waffles or crêpes. It makes a terrific topping on ice cream and desserts, too.

2 pounds peaches, peeled and pitted

½ cup organic cane sugar

2 tablespoons freshly squeezed lemon juice

1 teaspoon lemon zest

¼ teaspoon ground cardamom

Place all the ingredients in a medium saucepan and bring to a low boil over medium-high heat. Reduce the heat to medium and continue to cook for 20 minutes, stirring frequently.

Allow the mixture to cool for 5 minutes. Put it in the blender and pulse two or three times. Serve immediately.

CHAPTER 6
Dips and Salsas

The blender certainly comes in handy when it comes to entertaining.
Within minutes, you can have a table full of spicy salsas and satisfying dips that will
be more flavorful and nutritious than store-bought spreads, especially because you
can alter these recipes to suit *your* tastes. Just a little more mango and eliminate the
cilantro. Yes, more sesame oil please. Whatever your preference, make the recipe as
written, then make adjustments for your taste, little by little. A pinch of something
goes a long way in the blender.

Dips never go out of style. They are universally loved. They can get a party
started or turn some simple vegetables into a leisurely picnic. They can be made in
advance and feed plenty of guests.

Many of these recipes work as sandwich spreads, too. A thick smear of smoky
hummus layered with crunchy vegetables on hearty 12-grain bread makes a delectable lunch, as does a warm, crusty baguette topped with roasted garlic bean dip,
cherry-red tomatoes, and vibrant green arugula.

Fresh Pineapple Mango Salsa

makes **2 cups**

This salsa sings summer. It reminds me of eating dinner outside on the patio with candles flickering just after sunset. On the menu: Grilled fish tacos. A warm corn tortilla stuffed with grilled tilapia, shredded cabbage, a scoop of guac, and a nice big spoonful of Pineapple Mango Salsa. It makes my mouth water just thinking about it.

1-inch piece of gingerroot, peeled

½ jalapeño, seeded and cut in half

2 tablespoons freshly squeezed lime juice

1 ripe mango, peeled and cut into large chunks (about 1 cup)

½ pineapple, peeled and cut into chunks (2 heaping cups)

¼ cup fresh mint leaves

Put the ginger, jalapeño, and lime juice in the blender and run for 10 seconds on medium. Using a spatula, push the ingredients toward the blade.

Add the mango, pineapple, and mint to the blender and pulse three or four more times. The salsa should be somewhat chunky.

Simply Guac

makes about 2 cups

My husband is an ever-so-diligent guacamole maker. He grinds the garlic and salt into a paste, finely chops the onion and cilantro, and carefully smashes the avocados by hand. The result is outstanding but the method definitely takes effort.

Without sounding like an infomercial, you can achieve something pretty comparable in mere minutes. Yup, you know it. The blender. Just pulse ever-so-gingerly and you've got it, Simply Guac.

1 garlic clove, peeled

¼ cup fresh cilantro leaves

¼ small red onion, cut into chunks (about ¼ cup)

½ jalapeño, or more to taste, seeded and cut in half (about 2 teaspoons)

2 tablespoons freshly squeezed lime juice

½ teaspoon kosher salt

½ small tomato, cut in half and seeded

3 avocados, peeled, pitted, and cut in half

Put the garlic, cilantro, onion, jalapeño, lime juice, and salt in the blender and pulse two or three times.

Add the tomato and the avocado and pulse two more times. Garnish with a few cilantro leaves before serving.

Piquant Tomato and Chipotle Salsa (rear) and Simply Guac

Piquant Tomato and Chipotle Salsa

makes about 3 cups

No need to reserve this salsa for chips. Use it on omelets, mix it in with black beans, or even toss it with steamed veggies.

¼ cup coarsely chopped onion

¼ cup fresh cilantro leaves

1 teaspoon freshly squeezed lemon juice

3 to 4 medium tomatoes (about 24 ounces fresh tomatoes), cut into quarters

2 canned chipotle peppers (about 1 tablespoon each)

½ teaspoon kosher salt

Put the onion, cilantro, and lemon juice in the blender and pulse on low two times. Using a spatula, push the ingredients toward the blade.

Add the tomatoes, peppers, and salt, and blend for 5 seconds on medium. Do not overmix. Drain off a little liquid if needed and serve.

Roasted Garlic White Bean Dip

makes 1½ cups

The comforting flavors of this dip wrap around you like a warm blanket, leaving you feeling content and satisfied. Try it as a sandwich spread or pasta sauce, too.

1 head garlic

1 teaspoon extra-virgin olive oil

3 cups cooked white or cannellini beans, or 2 (15-ounce) cans beans, rinsed and drained

2 tablespoons fresh rosemary, plus an extra sprig or two for garnish

1 tablespoon flat-leaf parsley

2 tablespoons freshly squeezed lemon juice

¼ cup water

½ teaspoon kosher salt

½ teaspoon freshly ground pepper

Preheat the oven to 375°F. Cut the top off of the garlic head, place it on a piece of aluminum foil large enough to wrap around it, and drizzle with the olive oil. Wrap the foil around the garlic and roast for 45 minutes, or until the cloves are lightly browned. Allow it to cool slightly.

Remove the roasted garlic cloves from their skins (you can almost squeeze them out) and place them in the blender together with the rest of the ingredients.

Blend on medium about 10 seconds, or until combined. Garnish with fresh rosemary sprigs and serve.

Irresistible Blue Cheese Dip

makes about ¾ cup

This solid standby is de rigueur for any party foods repertoire. It is versatile and appeals to most everyone. Serve it with wings, cut veggies, or even topping a small round of beef filet on a slice of baguette. You can even thin it out with a little cream or buttermilk for a tasty salad dressing.

1 shallot, peeled and cut in half

1 tablespoon red wine vinegar

¼ cup sour cream

¼ cup mayonnaise, aïoli, or vegannaise

½ cup crumbled blue cheese

½ teaspoon freshly ground pepper

¼ teaspoon kosher salt

Put the shallot and red wine vinegar in the blender and process on medium for 20 seconds. Using a spatula, scrape the sides and push the shallot toward the blender blade. Process again until finely chopped.

Add the sour cream and mayonnaise (or aïoli or vegannaise) and pulse several times.

Using a spatula, put the mixture in a bowl and stir in the blue cheese, pepper, and salt.

Super-Easy Edamame Dip

makes about 2 cups

Be sure to save a few edamame to garnish this scrumptious green dip that can easily be mistaken for guacamole. Even with the telltale beans on top, you're still likely to get a few quizzical looks. I can almost guarantee one guest will ask, "Just what exactly is in this dip?"

3 trimmed scallions, white parts only

1 garlic clove, peeled

2 cups shelled edamame, cooked

½ cup water

1 tablespoon freshly squeezed lime juice

2 tablespoons sesame oil

1 tablespoon white miso paste

1 teaspoon soy sauce

½ cup fresh cilantro leaves

½ teaspoon sriracha, if desired

Put the scallions and garlic clove in the blender container and pulse several times. Using a spatula, scrape the garlic and scallions down from the sides of the pitcher.

Add the rest of the ingredients listed above (sriracha if desired) and process until smooth. Add salt to taste.

from left to right (front): Smoky Hummus and Artichokes, Piquant Tomato and Chipotle Salsa, Simply Guac (back) Fresh Pineapple Mango Salsa, Super-Easy Edamame Dip

Cooling Cucumber Tzatziki

makes about 1 cup

This Greek sauce is a delicious side to grilled meats and is especially good with Lamb Pita Burgers (page 157).

1 garlic clove, peeled

¼ cucumber, cut into chunks

1 cup plain Greek yogurt

1 tablespoon freshly squeezed lemon juice or white wine vinegar

½ teaspoon dried oregano

½ teaspoon cumin

1 tablespoon fresh dill

¼ teaspoon kosher salt

⅛ teaspoon freshly ground pepper

Place the garlic clove in the blender pitcher and pulse once or twice.

Add the rest of the ingredients and pulse three or four times or until combined.

Mushroom Pâté

Woodsy and earthy, this tasty terrine makes an impressive vegetarian appetizer. Spread it on a warm, crusty piece of baguette and you'll leave your guests swooning. If you have leftover pâté, heat it up in a skillet with a little cream and chicken broth for a quick yet exquisite pasta sauce.

2 tablespoons extra-virgin olive oil, plus extra for oiling the ramekin

3 small shallots, peeled and sliced

2 garlic cloves, peeled and sliced

1½ pounds mixed fresh mushrooms, such as portobello, crimini, shiitake, and oyster

¼ cup flat-leaf parsley leaves

1 tablespoon fresh thyme

½ teaspoon kosher salt

⅛ teaspoon freshly ground black pepper

1 cup cashews, soaked for 2 hours and drained

½ teaspoon freshly squeezed lemon juice

Heat the oil in a skillet over medium heat and add the shallots, sautéing them for 5 minutes. Then add the garlic, mushrooms, parsley, thyme, salt, and pepper, and sauté for another 5 minutes.

Transfer the mushroom mixture to the blender and add the cashews and lemon juice. Pulse several times until the mixture is combined but some texture still remains. Spoon into a well-oiled ramekin and cover tightly with plastic wrap. Chill for at least 2 hours or overnight. Serve on warm baguette rounds.

Smoky Hummus with Artichokes

makes about 4 cups

Paper or plastic? Canned or dried? Is there a right answer? I can't really say. I do know that they all have their advantages. The biggest one to canned beans is the fast factor. You can decide you want hummus one minute and the next it's in front of you, ready to be devoured.

Dried beans take more planning, but I do think their taste and texture are superior. There are numerous other benefits to dried beans (more cost-effective, less packaging, et cetera), but don't let those keep you from eating canned beans, which have all the nutritional value of dried.

As for paper or plastic? I guess I'll just avoid the question and take my own bags.

1 small garlic clove, peeled

1 cup dried chickpeas, cooked and peeled, or 2 (15-ounce) cans beans, rinsed and drained

½ cup cooking water or liquid from the canned chickpeas

¼ teaspoon cayenne pepper

1 teaspoon smoked paprika

⅓ cup tahini

1½ tablespoons freshly squeezed lemon juice

¼ cup extra-virgin olive oil

1 teaspoon kosher salt

1 (14-ounce) can artichoke hearts, drained

Put the garlic in the blender and pulse one or two times.

Add the rest of the ingredients except for the artichokes and process on medium speed for 30 seconds.

Add the artichokes and pulse three or four more times. Do not overprocess; you want some artichoke pieces to remain for texture.

Basic Aïoli

Yellow and rich, this homemade garlic mayonnaise can be served as a condiment with fish, vegetables, or really almost anything that is enhanced by the flavors of garlic and olive oil.

1 garlic clove, peeled
2 large egg yolks
½ teaspoon kosher salt
1 teaspoon lemon juice
2 tablespoons water, divided
¼ cup canola or grapeseed oil
½ cup extra-virgin olive oil

Put the garlic clove, egg yolks, salt, lemon juice, and 1 tablespoon water in the blender jar and process on medium for 5 seconds. Using a spatula, scrape the sides of the blender and push the ingredients toward the blade.

Next, remove the plug from the center of the blender lid and with the blender running on medium, slowly pour the canola oil drop by drop through the lid. You may want to use your hand as a shield so the mixture doesn't splatter all over. Continue adding all the canola oil this way. It should take about two minutes.

Add the second tablespoon of water and blend on medium for 5 seconds. Begin adding the olive oil drop by drop as well. Once the mixture starts to emulsify, you may pour the remaining oil in a steady stream until all of it is incorporated. Refrigerate until ready for use, up to 3 days.

CHAPTER 7

Soups

Soups, like smoothies, are a given when it comes to the blender. In fact, no other kitchen appliance comes close to achieving the velvety smooth texture a blender does. An immersion blender does an okay job, but the difference is detectable, and it usually makes a mess.

The blender can also make hot soup in minutes from whole vegetables—unbelievable, I know! The friction of the blades creates heat that warms the blender jar's contents as it runs. While you can make most soups this way—broccoli, squash, kale—I like to roast my ingredients first for a deeper, richer flavor. It's amazing what a mere half hour in the oven can do for veggies. They start to caramelize, and the heat brings out a sweet, nutty taste.

This chapter contains hearty soups as well as some lighter summer purees. Eating soups year-round is an exceptional way to pack nutrition into a meal. Whether you serve soup as a meal's starter or highlight it as the main course, you can easily count two servings of vegetables into your daily requirements.

Chicken and vegetable stocks serve as the base for most of these soups. If possible, make them homemade—then you know *everything* you're putting in your soup is good and pure, with no unnecessary additives. The clean flavor of the stock will only accentuate the soup's star ingredients, giving them the prominence they deserve.

You'll also see that most of the recipes make at least six servings. These quantities are purposefully large, which allows you to freeze portions for later if you don't eat up the soup right away. It's just like putting money in the bank!

Verdant Spring Pea Soup

serves 4

Freshly shelled peas are exquisite. There's something so wonderful about breaking open the pod to find those plump green jewels inside. Frozen peas are certainly a fine substitute, though, and will save you time. Whether you opt for fresh or frozen, this vitamin-C-rich soup highlights the essence of green peas because there is little to mask their naturally sweet flavor, only ingredients to enhance it—and it can be made in a jiffy. There's no doubt you'll get requests for second helpings, yes peas!

2 tablespoons extra-virgin olive oil

2 leeks, trimmed and sliced

1 shallot, peeled and sliced

1 garlic clove, peeled and sliced

3 cups spring- or filtered water

4 cups shelled peas, or 2 (10-ounce) bags frozen peas

¼ cup fresh mint

1 teaspoon fresh tarragon

½ teaspoon kosher salt

Crème fraîche or yogurt, chives, and olive oil for serving

Freshly ground black pepper to taste

Heat the olive oil in a Dutch oven over medium-high heat. Add the leeks, shallot, and garlic, and sauté for 5 to 8 minutes or until softened.

Add the water, peas, mint, tarragon, and salt. Bring to a simmer and cook for 5 minutes. Turn off the heat and allow the soup to cool for a few minutes.

Using a ladle, transfer the soup to the blender jar and puree, in two batches if necessary. Blend on medium for 20 seconds then high for 1 minute. Do not fill the blender jar more than three-quarters full.

Return the soup to the Dutch oven to gently heat it through again if necessary. Serve warm with a dollop of crème fraîche or yogurt, chives, a drizzle of olive oil, and a sprinkle of freshly ground black pepper.

Autumn Squash and Pear Soup

serves 6

Slightly sweet from the addition of pear, this beautiful golden soup says autumn like no other. You'll get a good healthy dose of beta-carotene and vitamin C from a bowlful, as well as a very happy belly.

3 acorn or 2 buttercup squash (or any assorted fall squash), about 4 pounds total, cut in half or quarters and seeded

2 tablespoons extra-virgin olive oil, divided

3 carrots, peeled and cut into 2-inch chunks

1 medium onion, sliced

4 cups (32 ounces) chicken broth, divided

2 pears, any variety, peeled and cored, cut into quarters

1 teaspoon kosher salt

¼ teaspoon freshly ground pepper

¼ teaspoon ground cinnamon

maple syrup for serving

Preheat the oven to 375°F. Place the squash cut-side up on a baking sheet lined with parchment paper and drizzle with 1 tablespoon of the oil. Bake for 1 hour.

Meanwhile, heat the second tablespoon of olive oil in a Dutch oven over medium-high heat. Add the carrots and onion and sauté for about 8 minutes or until the onion is softened. Set aside.

When the squash is fully cooked and cooled enough to handle, scoop it out of the skin and put half of it in the blender.

Add 2 cups of the broth, pears, carrots, onion, salt, pepper, and cinnamon, in that order.

Start the blender on low and process for 10 seconds, turning it to high and processing until velvety smooth. Return the blended soup to the Dutch oven. Next process the remaining squash and broth until smooth and add that to the pot as well. Warm the pureed soup on the stove top until heated through. Serve with a drizzle of maple syrup.

Hearty Kale and Potato Soup

serves 6–8

I apologize if you're tired of hearing me say blend lightly, *but I have to underscore the importance of it once more with this recipe. Potatoes can easily turn to glue in the blender. When blended with diligence, this soup is thick and rewarding. The addition of kale after blending gives a delightful toothsome texture to the soup.*

2 tablespoons extra-virgin olive oil

1 onion, coarsely chopped (about 1¼ cups)

1 garlic clove, sliced

3 large baking potatoes (about 2¼ pounds total), peeled and cut into large chunks

7 cups chicken broth, divided

3–4 cups kale (about 4 large leaves), stems removed and coarsely chopped

¾ pound cooked kielbasa sausage, cut into ¾-inch thick rounds

½ teaspoon freshly-ground black pepper

1½ teaspoons kosher salt

Heat the olive oil in a Dutch oven over medium-high heat. Add the onion and garlic and sauté 5 to 8 minutes or until softened. Add the potatoes and sauté another 3 minutes, stirring frequently. Pour in 6 cups of the broth and bring to a boil. Reduce the heat and simmer for 15 minutes.

When the potatoes are cooked through, pour the soup in the blender and pulse three or four times on high or until almost smooth, in two batches if necessary. Do not process for more than 30 seconds as the soup will become gummy.

Pour the soup back in the Dutch oven, adding the kale, sausage, and remaining 1 cup broth, pepper, and salt. Simmer for another 10 minutes, until the kale has softened and the sausage is heated through.

Chicken Tortilla Soup

serves 6

Seems like a lot of steps here doesn't it? Okay, I admit it, this soup may be more time consuming than the others but the reward is great. If you want to shorten the process, buy a rotisserie chicken to shred. Then go straight to the soaking chile step. Now does it seem more doable? I hope so. I'd hate for you to pass up this flavorful, slightly fiery soup.

7 cups chicken broth, divided

1¼ pounds boneless chicken breasts

2 dried New Mexico chiles or red Anaheim-type chiles, stemmed and seeded

8 (6-inch) corn tortillas, divided

3 tablespoons canola oil or aroma-free coconut oil, divided

1 yellow onion, diced

3 garlic cloves, peeled and minced

4 teaspoons chili powder, divided

2 teaspoons ground cumin

½ teaspoon ground coriander

1 teaspoon kosher salt, divided

3 cups diced fire-roasted tomatoes, such as Muir Glen Organic brand

1 bay leaf

¼ cup cilantro

Freshly ground black pepper to taste

Diced avocado, queso fresco, and lime, for garnish

Bring 3 cups of the chicken broth to a boil in a large Dutch oven. When the broth comes to boil, gently lower the chicken breasts into the pot. Bring the liquid back to a gentle boil, then turn down the heat to low to maintain a simmer with the pot uncovered. Make sure the breasts are covered with broth. If necessary, add water until the chicken is completely submerged.

After about 10 minutes, turn the heat off, cover the pot, and allow the chicken to sit in the hot liquid for another 10 minutes. After that time, remove one of the breasts and check it for doneness by cutting into the center of the breast. If it's pink, it is not done and you should return it to the broth until it's cooked through. Remove the cooked breasts to a plate and cover with foil to cool.

Next, using your hands break up the chiles into a bowl filled with hot water (not boiling). Allow the chiles to soak for 15 minutes. Meanwhile, cut six of the tortillas into 3-inch-long by ½-inch-wide strips. Heat 2 tablespoons of the oil in a Dutch oven over medium-high heat. Add the tortilla strips to the hot oil and fry them for about a minute, gently tossing them to prevent burning. When they're golden, transfer them to a paper-towel-lined plate to drain. Set aside.

Reduce the heat to medium, add the remaining 1 tablespoon oil, stir in the onion and garlic, and sauté for about 8 minutes or until softened. Add 3 teaspoons of the chili powder along with the cumin, coriander, and ½ teaspoon of the salt; stir well. Cook the mixture for another minute or so.

Add the remaining 4 cups of chicken broth as well as the tomatoes, bay leaf, cilantro, and remaining two tortillas, torn into 1-inch pieces; stir together. Bring to a gentle boil then reduce the heat and simmer for 15 minutes.

While the soup is simmering, shred the still-warm chicken using two forks. Hold a breast firmly with one fork while you tear the chicken apart into shredded pieces with the other. Continue to do this until all the chicken is shredded. Sprinkle the remaining 1 teaspoon chili powder and ½ teaspoon salt over the chicken; toss it to coat.

After 15 minutes of cooking time, allow the soup to cool for 5 minutes then use a ladle to transfer half of it to the blender jar, add the drained soaked chiles, and pulse several times. Do not fill the blender jar more than three-quarters full.

Return the pureed soup to the Dutch oven and add the chicken. Turn the heat to medium and simmer until the chicken is warmed through. Season with the pepper.

Serve with the fried tortilla strips, avocado, queso fresco, and a squeeze of lime.

Spicy Chickpea Soup

serves 6

Rich with the flavor of chickpeas, this homey, satiating soup includes fire-roasted tomatoes and paprika for a vibrant spice. It's the kind of soup you want to dip a thick, gooey grilled cheese into.

3 tablespoons extra-virgin olive oil

2 garlic cloves, finely diced

1 large onion, peeled and cut into medium dice

2 teaspoons smoked paprika

1 teaspoon ground cumin

½ teaspoon turmeric

½ teaspoon kosher salt

1 (28-ounce) can diced fire-roasted tomatoes, such as Muir Glen

2 (15-ounce) cans chickpeas, rinsed and drained

4 cups chicken broth

Salt and freshly ground pepper to taste

¼ cup flat-leaf parsley, finely chopped, for garnish

Lemon zest, for garnish

Heat the oil over medium heat in a large soup pot or Dutch oven. Sauté the garlic and onion for 8 to 10 minutes or until softened. Add the spices and seasonings and sauté for another 2 minutes.

Add the tomatoes, chickpeas, and broth. Simmer for 5 minutes.

Using a ladle, spoon half the soup into the blender jar and process for 45 seconds on medium. Pour the pureed soup back into the pot and stir together. Add salt and pepper to taste.

Heat through and serve with chopped parsley and lemon zest for garnish.

Comforting Broccoli Leek Soup

serves 6

A lighter version of broccoli cheddar soup, this cream-less blend is equally rewarding. The addition of potato gives the base a velvety texture, and a sprinkle of cheddar cheese helps you avoid of any feelings of deprivation.

2 tablespoons extra-virgin olive oil

1 cup leeks, sliced

1 carrot, peeled and cut into 2-inch chunks

2 garlic cloves, peeled and cut in half

1 (8-ounce) russet (baking) potato, peeled and cut into 2-inch cubes (about 1 heaping cup)

½ teaspoon kosher salt

4 cups (32 ounces) vegetable stock

1 (2-pound) head broccoli, cut into florets (about 7 cups)

1 cup shredded cheddar cheese (4 ounces)

Heat the olive oil in a Dutch oven over medium-high heat. Sauté the leeks and carrot for 6 minutes.

Reduce the heat to medium-low, add the garlic, and sauté another 2 minutes. Next add the potato, sprinkle with the salt, sauté 2 more minutes, then add the vegetable stock and bring to a boil.

Reduce the heat and simmer the stock mixture for 10 minutes. Add the broccoli and simmer for 10 more minutes.

Transfer the soup to the blender and process on high until smooth. Salt and pepper to taste. Reheat if necessary and serve with shredded cheddar cheese sprinkled over each serving.

Creamy Cauliflower Fennel Soup with Parmesan Gremolata

serves **6**

The roasted vegetables in this soup are so fragrant and tempting, you may want to eat them straight off the baking tray. It's hard not to snag a few, but you won't regret blending them into a pleasing puree.

2 tablespoons extra-virgin olive oil

1 tablespoon freshly squeezed lemon juice

1 head cauliflower, cut into florets (about 6 cups)

1 head fennel, coarsely chopped (about 2 heaping cups)

1 small onion, coarsely chopped (about 1½ cups)

2 garlic cloves, peeled

4 cups (32 ounces) vegetable or chicken broth

Kosher salt and freshly ground pepper to taste

Parmesan Gremolata (below)

Preheat the oven to 400°F. Combine the olive oil and lemon juice in a small bowl. Spread the cauliflower, fennel, onion, and garlic cloves on a baking sheet (or two if needed so everything is in a single layer). Toss with the oil-lemon mixture and roast for 20 minutes.

After 20 minutes, use a spatula to toss the mixture on the baking sheets and roast it for another 20 minutes. Meanwhile, pour the broth in the blender pitcher; when the vegetables are done roasting, scrape all the vegetables on the baking sheets into the blender pitcher as well. Process on high until smooth, about 2 minutes.

Heat soup on a stove top and add salt and pepper to taste. Sprinkle with Parmesan Gremolata.

Parmesan Gremolata

2 tablespoons fresh rosemary leaves

1 tablespoon lemon zest

1 garlic clove, peeled

3 tablespoons grated Parmesan cheese

Place all the ingredients in the blender and process on low for 15 seconds. Scrape down the sides of the blender and repeat if necessary. Sprinkle over Creamy Cauliflower Fennel Soup.

Green Gazpacho

serves **6**

While many think of gazpacho as a spicy tomato-based soup, there are many variations to be found in Spain, its origin country, and this is one of them. Inspired by summer's bountiful harvest, this tomato-less soup combines a plethora of healthy green veggies. Serve it cold in shot glasses or in a small mug for a cheerful presentation.

2 cucumbers, seeded and cut into large chunks (about 3 cups)

1 small zucchini, cut into large chunks (about 1 heaping cup)

1 cup shelled peas, blanched

½ small yellow onion, coarsely chopped (about ¾ cup)

1 green bell pepper, seeds removed, cut into quarters

3 tablespoons freshly squeezed lemon juice

¼ cup extra-virgin olive oil

2 tablespoons white wine vinegar

1 teaspoon organic cane sugar

1 teaspoon kosher salt

1 garlic clove

¼ teaspoon ground coriander

1 teaspoon ground cumin

Pinch of freshly ground white pepper

1–2 cups springwater or filtered tap water

Plain Greek yogurt and freshly cut chives, for garnish

Place all the ingredients (except the yogurt and chives) in the blender in the order listed. Process on low for 20 seconds, then turn to high and run on high until velvety smooth.

Chill for at least 2 hours and serve with a small dollop of plain Greek yogurt and freshly cut chives.

CHAPTER 8

Salads

A salad in the blender? *Really?* Yup, it's no joke. The whirring blade makes a mean chopped kale salad in minutes. However, most delicate lettuce leaves don't stand up to the machine's power. Homemade salad dressings do, though. A blender is very useful when making creamy vinaigrettes and emulsions.

A good salad dressing enhances ingredients, adding another dimension to fresh fruits and vegetables. Like everything else you make in the blender, when you make your own salad dressings, you control all the ingredients that go into it. What can start out as a healthy, organic salad can turn into a sugar-laden, chemical-ridden meal when you use store-bought dressings. Steer clear of those bottled concoctions and go for your own blend.

Another benefit: You'll save money. You can make just the amount you need, or will use in the following week, and forgo opening a large bottle that goes half uneaten and ends up in the trash.

These salads go beyond lettuce and incorporate quinoa, lentils, and heartier vegetables for a more adequate meal. You can always add a protein—chicken, shrimp, pork—for something even more hardy. The inclusion of heart-healthy fats, fiber-rich nuts, and nutrient-dense seeds turns these simple salads into super-charged meals.

Spinach Salad with Blueberry Vinaigrette

serves 4

It seems the nutritional benefits of blueberries are being touted today more than ever. A couple of handfuls added to a vinaigrette and a few more tossed with this salad will boost your vitamin C and antioxidant intake. Do you really need more reason, though, than their sweet juicy taste?

For the vinaigrette

¾ cup fresh blueberries
¼ cup balsamic vinegar
⅓ cup extra-virgin olive oil
1 teaspoon Dijon mustard
½ teaspoon kosher salt
1 teaspoon organic cane sugar

For the salad

½ cup pecans
1 (5-ounce) bag baby spinach
2 heads endive, sliced
1 carrot, peeled and grated
⅓ cup whole fresh blueberries
½ cup crumbled goat cheese

Mix all the vinaigrette ingredients together in the blender until smooth.

Heat the pecans in a small skillet over medium heat, stirring constantly for several minutes until they darken and become toasted. Remove from the stovetop and allow to cool.

Toss the spinach leaves, endive, carrots, blueberries, and cooled pecans with the Blueberry Vinaigrette. Sprinkle with the crumbled goat cheese. Save the remaining vinaigrette refrigerated for up to 5 days.

Chopped Kale Salad

serves 4–6

This salad is substantial, as are the parts that make it. Not all salad leaves can withstand the power of the blender, but kale can. Remove the ribs, add the leaves to your blender jar with water, and your blades will do all the work. You'll need to repeat this action several times for each vegetable added to the salad—they take different times to dice up, and you'll need to drain each element thoroughly—but it's worth it. The result is a crunchy, uniformly chopped salad.

For the salad

¾ cup pine nuts

1 bunch kale, ribs and stems removed

2 carrots, peeled and cut into 2-inch chunks

6 radishes, cut in half

2 ounces blue cheese, crumbled (about 3 heaping tablespoons)

For the dressing

1 garlic clove, peeled

½ avocado, pitted and peeled

¼ cup freshly squeezed lemon juice (juice of about 2 lemons)

1 tablespoon Dijon mustard

2 tablespoons water

1 tablespoon raw honey

½ cup extra-virgin olive oil

Put the pine nuts in a skillet and toast for about 5 minutes over medium heat, stirring constantly. Set aside to cool.

Next, put the kale in the blender and add 4 cups of water. Pulse 8 to 10 times with short, quick pulses. Drain the greens and put them in a large salad bowl lined with paper towels.

Add the carrots and radishes to the blender and fill with enough water to cover the vegetables. Pulse several times until chopped, drain, and add to the salad bowl.

To make the dressing: Place the garlic in the blender jar and pulse several times. Add the rest of the ingredients, except the olive oil. Process on high for 30 seconds. Add the oil and continue to blend until thoroughly mixed.

Remove the paper towel from the bottom of the bowl and toss the salad with the dressing and pine nuts. Sprinkle with the blue cheese. Toss a few more times and serve.

Classic Caesar Salad with Homemade Garlic Croutons

I first learned to make a Caesar when I was living with my sister one summer while I was in college. She made me a garlicky salad that blew me away. Shortly thereafter she gave me explicit directions for how to make it. The key was pouring the olive oil in a slow, thin stream so the dressing would emulsify.

Some things just never go out of style, and a classic Caesar is one of them. My kids love this salad as much today as I did 20 years ago. One caveat: They like it when I replace the lemon juice with balsamic vinegar. That's their little twist on a beloved classic.

For the salad

1 garlic clove, peeled

1 anchovy or ½ teaspoon kosher salt

2 large egg yolks

1 teaspoon Dijon mustard

1 teaspoon Worcestershire sauce

2 tablespoons freshly squeezed lemon juice

½ cup extra-virgin olive oil

2 heads romaine lettuce, washed, dried, and torn into bite-sized pieces

½ cup freshly grated Parmesan cheese

Freshly ground black pepper

For the croutons

2 tablespoons plus 1 teaspoon extra-virgin olive oil

1 garlic clove, sliced

3 slices sourdough bread, cut into 1-inch cubes (about 2 heaping cups)

Put the garlic in the blender and run on high for 5 seconds. Add the anchovy or salt, egg yolks, Dijon mustard, Worcestershire, and lemon juice, and run on high for 10 more seconds. Scrape all the ingredients down toward the blade with a spatula.

While running the blender on low, slowly pour the olive oil through the opening in the lid and blend until slightly thickened.

Make the croutons: Heat the 2 tablespoons oil in a skillet over medium-high heat. Add the bread and stir constantly for about 3 minutes. Add the remaining teaspoon oil and the garlic and continue to stir, toasting the bread for another two minutes, or until the bread cubes are toasted and golden brown.

Toss the lettuce leaves, Parmesan, pepper, and croutons with the dressing just before serving.

Bibb Lettuce with Grapefruit Shallot Vinaigrette

serves 4

The sweet and tart dressing here lightly coats the delicate Bibb leaves of this salad, which are balanced by the slight crunch of sunflower seed kernels. While this salad shines as a side, it becomes a star when topped with grilled shrimp and served as a main course.

2 shallots, peeled and sliced (about ¼ cup)

½ cup plus 1 tablespoon extra-virgin olive oil

⅓ cup plus 1 tablespoon grapefruit juice

1 teaspoon organic cane sugar

1 teaspoon Dijon mustard

1 tablespoon orange marmalade

1 teaspoon fresh rosemary

½ teaspoon kosher salt

¼ teaspoon freshly ground black pepper

1 head Bibb lettuce

1 grapefruit, peeled and cut into segments

½ cup ricotta salata (1 ounce), shaved with a vegetable peeler

¼ cup hulled sunflower seeds

In a small saucepan, sauté the shallots in 1 tablespoon of the olive oil for about 4 minutes. Sprinkle with 1 tablespoon of the grapefruit juice and the teaspoon of sugar. Cook on low for 8 to 10 minutes.

Whisk in the the rest of the grapefruit juice and mustard to the shallot mixture and cook over medium-high heat until it comes to a gentle boil. Stir in the orange marmalade, rosemary, salt, and pepper; cook for another minute.

Transfer the mixture to the blender, add the remaining ½ cup olive oil, and process for 1 minute or until smooth. Toss with the Bibb lettuce, grapefruit segments, ricotta salata, and sunflower seeds, and serve. Save the remaining vinaigrette, if any, refrigerated for up to 5 days.

Summer Corn and Avocado Salad with Cilantro Buttermilk Dressing

serves 4

There's nothing like sweet, crunchy corn cut right off the cob—and tossing it with avocado and a creamy buttermilk dressing takes the deliciousness to an even higher elevation. To stretch this salad a little further, add in a few cups of arugula leaves.

For the dressing

1 small shallot, peeled and cut in half

¼ cup buttermilk

¼ cup mayonnaise

2 tablespoons extra-virgin olive oil

¼ cup fresh cilantro leaves

1 tablespoon white wine vinegar

½ teaspoon kosher salt

½ teaspoon freshly ground black pepper

For the salad

4 ears corn, shucked and boiled

3 green onions, sliced

1 avocado, peeled, pitted, and cut into ½-inch cubes

smoked paprika for serving (optional)

Pulse the shallot in the blender several times. Add the rest of the ingredients for the dressing to the blender and process on high for 1 minute. Set aside.

Cut the kernels off the corn cobs and put in a medium-sized bowl. Add the green onions and avocado. Toss with the Cilantro Buttermilk Dressing. Season to taste with salt, pepper, and smoked paprika if desired. Serve cold or at room temperature. Save the remaining dressing, refrigerated, for up to 3 days.

Carrot Quinoa Salad

serves 4

Quinoa is a quick and easy way to add protein to a salad. It's also gluten-free and deeply gratifying. This salad holds well and makes a great lunch-on-the-go.

For the salad

1 cup quinoa

2 cups diced carrots (about 1 pound)

2 teaspoons extra-virgin olive oil

¼ teaspoon kosher salt

For the dressing

1 tablespoon tahini

1 tablespoon soy sauce

1 tablespoon freshly squeezed lemon juice

1 tablespoon sesame oil

¼ teaspoon sriracha

1 tablespoon water

1 bunch scallions, trimmed and cut into 2-inch pieces (about 5)

Rinse and cook the quinoa according to the package's instructions. Meanwhile, preheat the oven to 400°F. Place the diced carrots on a baking sheet and toss with the olive oil and salt. Roast the carrots for 15 minutes, tossing twice during that time.

To make the dressing, place all the ingredients minus one scallion in the blender pitcher and process for 1 minute on high.

Toss the cooked quinoa and carrots with the dressing and chop the remaining scallion for garnish.

French Lentil Salad with Roasted Tomato Vinaigrette

serves 4

Slow-roasted tomatoes are sweet and addictive. You may want to double the amount you roast so you can have extras to snack on. The fragrant smell of the roasting onions and tomatoes always gets my kids in the kitchen asking, "What are you cooking, Mom?" They usually stay pretty close by until the salad is tossed up.

For the salad

1 pint cherry tomatoes, cut in half

½ large red onion, sliced (about 1½ cups)

1 tablespoon extra-virgin olive oil

1 tablespoon balsamic vinegar

1 teaspoon organic cane sugar

1 cup green lentils, rinsed

1 bay leaf

1 garlic clove, peeled

1 carrot, washed and cut into 2-inch chunks

3 cups arugula

½ cup crumbled feta cheese

For the vinaigrette

3 tablespoons extra-virgin olive oil

2 tablespoons balsamic vinegar

¾ teaspoon kosher salt

Preheat the oven to 350°F. Line a baking sheet with parchment paper. Place the tomatoes and onion in a bowl and toss with the oil, balsamic, and sugar. Spread them evenly on the pan, flat-side down, and bake for 25 minutes.

Meanwhile, put the lentils, bay leaf, garlic clove, and carrot in a saucepan and cover with 2 inches of water. Bring to a boil. Simmer over moderate heat about 30 minutes, or until the lentils are tender.

To make the vinaigrette: While the lentils are cooking, place ¼ cup of the roasted tomatoes in the blender with the oil, vinegar, and salt. Blend on high for 30 seconds or until thoroughly combined.

Drain any excess water from the lentils, remove the bay leaf, carrot, and garlic, and put in a bowl with the remaining ¾ cup of tomatoes, roasted onion, arugula, and feta.

Toss with the vinaigrette and serve.

Go-To Herb Vinaigrette

makes about ½ cup

How is it that the French can make simple salad greens taste so splendid? Every time? I find the majority of restaurants in France, from the north to south, serve a small handful of dressed greens with the sheerest vinaigrette that is consistently ever-so-tantalizing. What is it, then, that makes a French vinaigrette authentic? Perhaps it's the quality of the olive oil and Dijon, or the fresh, delicate herbs. We'll call this blend my "Ffrench" vinaigrette. It's my daily go-to salad dressing. Hopefully it'll beckon you to eat your greens like those blends in France do.

1 small shallot, peeled
2 tablespoons red wine vinegar
½ teaspoon kosher salt
¼ teaspoon freshly ground black pepper
¼ teaspoon organic cane sugar
1 teaspoon Dijon mustard
2 teaspoons fresh tarragon
2 teaspoons fresh thyme
1 teaspoon fresh oregano
⅓ cup extra-virgin olive oil

Put the shallot in the blender and run on high for 10 seconds. Scrape the shallot off the sides of the blender toward the blade using a spatula.

Add the vinegar, salt, pepper, sugar, and mustard. Process again on medium for another 20 seconds.

Add the herbs and process again for 10 seconds.

Lastly, add the olive oil and run the blender for 1 minute on high or until the dressing is thoroughly combined and the herbs are finely chopped. Stop the blender and scrape down the sides as necessary. Serve over mesclun or other desired greens.

CHAPTER 9

Blender Burgers

I'm not sure when my zeal for blender burgers started, but boy oh boy do I love them. And my family does, too. The blender quickly combines an array of ingredients that can be formed into patties and cooked up in no time. Add a veggie side and dinner's done. What's not to love?

The salmon and lamb burgers are two of my favorites, but then again I always have a hankering for pork sliders, and the black bean burgers are a staple in our house. Truly, they're all very tasty. There are also many vegetarian options for a satiating meatless meal.

Vegetarian burgers should not be compared to meat burgers for texture or taste. These are not *faux* meat burgers, they are their own entity, teeming with the earthy flavor of vegetables, crunchy textures of grains, and some hint of spice.

Veggie burgers are not as firm as meat burgers, either, and should be handled delicately. Refrigerating the patties helps make them more manageable for cooking. (If you have time, refrigerate the burger mix before and after forming the patties.) Don't get discouraged if your burger falls apart on your first attempt. Turn up the heat and try again. A hot pan helps the binders in the burger congeal. Also ensure that your ingredients are as dry as possible at the outset: Drain beans well and squeeze out unnecessary moisture from the vegetables.

Serve burgers on buns, with salad, or even with just a dollop of dip such as tzatziki or guacamole. I hope one bite is enough to inspire the enthusiasm I have for this simple pleasure.

Family-Favorite Salmon Burgers with Quick Pickled Cukes

serves 4

These robust burgers will give beef burgers a run for their money any day—they are big, juicy, and flavorful just like a burger should be. Watercress adds a nice bite to the firm but not-too-firm texture. Since ketchup isn't an option here (or at least I hope not!), the Quick Pickled Cukes are a must. Their zesty crunch makes them the perfect condiment.

For the burgers

1 pound skinless, boneless salmon fillet, cut into large chunks

3 ounces smoked salmon

1 large egg

¾ cup watercress

1 teaspoon lemon zest

⅛ teaspoon freshly-ground black pepper

1 tablespoon extra-virgin olive oil

For the Quick Pickled Cukes

½ cup white vinegar

1 tablespoon organic cane sugar

¼ teaspoon crushed red pepper flakes

⅛ teaspoon kosher salt

1 whole cucumber, very thinly sliced

To make the cukes: Combine the vinegar, sugar, pepper flakes, and salt in a bowl; add the cucumber slices. Cover with plastic wrap and allow to marinate for at least 30 minutes before serving.

To make the burgers, place all the ingredients (except the oil) in the blender and pulse four to five times until just combined. The mixture should be chunky.

Form the mixture into four patties and place on waxed paper.

Heat the oil in a skillet over medium-high heat. Carefully slide the patties into the heated skillet and cook for about 4 minutes on each side or until heated through. Serve on buns with Quick Pickled Cukes.

Pork Burger Sliders with Tangy Barbecue Sauce

serves 4

We are big fans of sliders in our house. Is it because they're so cute? Because we feel like we're eating more? I'm not really sure, but we love them. In these sweet little gems, pork and beef are complemented by the smoky taste of bacon. Some cheddar and onion are thrown in. And don't forget the homemade Tangy Barbecue Sauce that tops these babies—you're sure to become a fan, too.

½ small red onion, cut into quarters (about ½ cup)

7 slices bacon (about 7 ounces), cut into quarters

¾ pound ground pork

¾ pound ground beef

2 ounces grated cheddar cheese (about ½ cup)

2 tablespoons Tangy Barbecue Sauce (recipe follows)

Plus extra barbecue sauce, cheddar cheese, and cooked bacon slices for topping the burgers

Put the onion and raw bacon in the blender and pulse three times. Using a spatula, push it toward the blade. Add the pork, beef, cheese, and barbecue sauce. Pulse several more times until just combined. Do not overblend. If needed, turn the mixture out onto a sheet of wax paper and knead with your hands. The meat should not become pasty from blending.

Using a ⅓-cup measure, make nine 3-ounce slider patties. Grill or pan-fry until cooked through. Top with extra cheddar cheese, Tangy Barbecue Sauce, and cooked bacon slices.

Tangy Barbecue Sauce

2 tablespoons extra-virgin olive oil

½ small sweet onion, cut into large chunks

4 cloves garlic, peeled and smashed

1½ teaspoons chipotle chili powder

1½ teaspoons ground cumin

1½ teaspoons dried oregano

1 teaspoon ground coriander

⅛ teaspoon ginger powder

1½ teaspoons Dijon mustard

½ teaspoon kosher salt

½ teaspoon freshly ground pepper

14-ounce bottle (1¼ cups) organic ketchup

3 tablespoons white vinegar or more to taste

2 tablespoons light brown sugar

1 teaspoon Liquid Smoke

Heat the oil in a 2-quart pot over medium-high heat. Add the onion and garlic and sauté for 8 to 10 minutes or until well softened.

Add the chili powder, cumin, oregano, coriander, ginger, Dijon, salt, and pepper. Stir continuously while still sautéing the mixture over medium-high heat.

Next, add the entire bottle of ketchup (don't throw out the bottle), and stir thoroughly. Bring the sauce to a gentle simmer then reduce the heat, continuing to stir until the ketchup starts to caramelize and brown, about 3 to 5 minutes.

Add the vinegar, brown sugar, and Liquid Smoke and stir well. Next, fill the ketchup bottle about ½ full with water (about ⅔ cup) and shake it up, pouring enough of the water into the sauce to make it the consistency of tomato soup. Heat through.

Using a ladle, transfer the sauce to the blender jar and process on medium for 15 seconds, then turn the power to high for another minute until the sauce is completely smooth.

This sauce will keep refrigerated for 1 month or frozen for up to 6 months.

Herbed Goat Cheese Turkey Burgers

serves 4–6

I know, I know. Turkey burgers can be bland and boring. I guarantee, though, these are not another ho-hum bird burger. Fresh herbs infuse lots of flavor into the meat, and a schmear of Herbed Goat Cheese adds even more character. To ensure a moist, full-flavored burger, look for organic, pasture-raised ground turkey with white and dark meat blended together (90 to 93 percent lean), steering away from ground turkey made from all-white breast meat, which tends to be dry.

For the Herbed Goat Cheese

2 tablespoons buttermilk

1 (4-ounce) log goat cheese

1 teaspoon fresh rosemary

1 teaspoon fresh sage

1 teaspoon fresh thyme

½ garlic clove

¼ teaspoon kosher salt

⅛ teaspoon freshly ground black pepper

For the burgers

2 tablespoons extra-virgin olive oil

¼ cup red onion, coarsely chopped

2 garlic cloves, peeled

½ serrano pepper, seeded and cut in half

⅓ cup loosely packed chopped flat-leaf parsley

2 tablespoons fresh rosemary

1 tablespoon fresh sage

2 tablespoons fresh thyme

1 teaspoon kosher salt

½ teaspoon freshly ground black pepper

1 large egg

2 pounds ground turkey meat

To make the Herbed Goat Cheese: Combine all the ingredients in the blender and run on medium until smooth and creamy. Stop the blender and use a spatula to scrape down the mixture from the sides and push it toward the blade several times if needed. Set aside.

To make the burgers: Add all the turkey burger ingredients except the ground meat to the blender and pulse several times until chopped and combined. Add the turkey and pulse two or three times until everything is just mixed together. Do not overprocess the meat.

Form the mixture into six patties and chill for 1 hour. Grill until cooked through. Serve with a dollop of Herbed Goat Cheese.

from left to right: Zesty Black Bean Burgers (front); Pork Burger Sliders, Herbed Goat Cheese Turkey Burgers (center); Tart Lemon Squares, Fudgy Gluten-Free Brownies, Green Gazpacho (rear)

Lamb Pita Burgers

serves 4

Like Salmon Burgers, Lamb Pitas are a regular in our dinner rotation. They come together quickly, my family loves them, and they make great leftovers. Pair a few lamb patties with lettuce leaves and a slice of tomato, add a dollop of tzatziki, and you've got a mouthwatering meal.

2 garlic cloves, peeled

2 tablespoons fresh mint

2 tablespoons fresh cilantro

2 tablespoons plain Greek yogurt

½ teaspoon cumin

½ teaspoon turmeric

¼ teaspoon kosher salt

⅛ teaspoon freshly ground black pepper

1½ pounds ground lamb

2 teaspoons extra-virgin olive oil

Whole wheat pitas

Chopped lettuce and tomatoes

Put the garlic, mint, and cilantro in the blender pitcher and pulse several times on medium, using a spatula as needed to scrape the sides.

Add the yogurt, cumin, turmeric, salt, pepper, and lamb. Pulse again three or four times or until just mixed.

Turn the mixture out onto a sheet of waxed paper, using a spatula to scrape all the meat out.

Using a tablespoon measure, form the mixture into small patties using 2 tablespoons per patty.

Once all the meat is formed into patties (you should get about 14), heat the oil in a cast-iron skillet or fry pan over medium-high heat.

When the pan is thoroughly preheated, cook the patties in batches, turning them with a spatula after several minutes. Once they're browned on all sides, turn down the heat and cook for another few minutes. Your total cooking time will be about 8 minutes. Serve in pitas with tomato, lettuce, and Cooling Cucumber Tzatziki (page 109).

Super-Satisfying Beet and Chickpea Burgers

serves 4–6

Don't let the list of ingredients here scare you. I know it seems long and perhaps daunting. With the help of the blender, though, everything gets mixed up in a snap. The balance of beans and vegetables and brown rice is important to achieving a vegetarian burger that's more than just mush. Dipping the burger in bread crumbs before frying gives a crispy golden crust to the patty.

4 tablespoons extra-virgin olive oil, divided

2 tablespoons balsamic vinegar

2 garlic cloves, peeled and cut in half

1 (6-ounce) beet, peeled and cut into chunks

3 carrots, peeled and cut into 2-inch chunks (about 1 generous cup)

1 large red onion, cut into large chunks (about 2 cups)

½ cup cooked brown rice

⅓ cup oat flour

1 large egg

1 teaspoon ground cumin

½ teaspoon ground coriander

3 cups cooked chickpeas or 2 (15-ounce) cans chickpeas, drained and rinsed

⅓ cup finely ground whole wheat bread crumbs

Goat cheese and mixed baby sprouts (available from farmer's markets), for garnish

Preheat the oven to 375°F. Put 2 tablespoons of the oil, along with the vinegar and garlic cloves, into the blender; process until combined. Put the beet, carrots, and onion on a baking sheet, toss with the oil-vinegar mixture, and roast for 35 minutes, tossing halfway through, or until the beet is fork-tender. Remove from the oven and allow to cool.

Put the roasted vegetables, brown rice, oat flour, egg, cumin, and coriander in the blender container and run on medium for 10 seconds. Using a spatula, push the ingredients toward the blade and run for another 10 seconds. Add the chickpeas and pulse another one or two times, until just combined.

Form the mixture into patties and chill for 1 hour.

Put the bread crumbs on a plate and, just before frying, lightly coat each patty. To fry, heat the remaining 2 tablespoons of oil over medium-high heat in a skillet. Gently slide the patties into the pan and cook for about 3 minutes on each side or until lightly golden brown. Top with a slice of goat cheese and sprouts to serve.

Zesty Black Bean Burgers

serves **4–6**

The spicy combination of ingredients in these patties puts them somewhere between a burrito and black bean dip. Fry them up in a hot pan so they're crisp, with an interior that's soft but not mushy, and you've got a black bean burger. I like to eat them on a salad and not a bun, but either way they'll fill you up.

1 garlic clove, peeled and cut into quarters

½ small red onion, peeled and cut into quarters (about ½ cup)

1 small jalapeño, seeded and cut into quarters

¼ cup fresh cilantro leaves

1 teaspoon lime zest

½ cup blue corn tortilla chips, crushed

½ cup sweet potato (about ½ large potato), cooked and mashed

3 cups cooked black beans, or 2 (15-ounce) cans black beans, rinsed and drained

1 large egg, plus 1 large egg white

1 teaspoon ground cumin

3 tablespoons grated cheddar cheese

¼ teaspoon kosher salt

2 tablespoons extra-virgin olive oil

Put the garlic, onion, jalapeño, cilantro, zest, and tortilla chips in the blender container. Pulse on medium three or four times or until the onion and garlic are finely minced. Use a spatula to push everything toward the blade between pulses. Add the sweet potato and process for 10 seconds on medium.

Add the beans, egg and egg white, cumin, cheese, and salt. Run the blender on low for 10 seconds or until combined. Use the spatula to stir everything together. You want to retain some whole beans and *not* let the mixture turn to a smooth puree.

Line a baking sheet with waxed paper. Make eight patties using a ⅓-cup measure. Scoop out the mixture onto the prepared pan and press down slightly with your hand or the bottom of the measuring cup. Place the patties in the freezer for at least 30 minutes.

When the patties are chilled, heat the olive oil in large skillet over medium-high heat. Gently slide as many patties as you can fit into the pan, with a couple of inches between each patty.

Cook the patties for 2 minutes on each side, flipping them very gently. Repeat by cooking them 1 more minute on each side (6 minutes total).

Serve on a bed of lettuce with a spoonful of Simply Guac (page 100) and Piquant Tomato and Chipotle Salsa (page 102).

Quinoa and Butternut Squash Burgers

serves 4–6

Filled with grains and veggies, these patties are soft and moist but still maintain a wonderful texture from the quinoa. The subtle hint of sage flavors these tender burgers that are smothered in melted Parmesan cheese and topped with oven-roasted onions, which makes them deeply satisfying.

½ butternut squash (about 1 pound), seeded and cut in half

1½ yellow onions, sliced

2 tablespoons extra-virgin olive oil, divided

¾ teaspoon kosher salt

1 egg

½ cup grated Parmesan cheese, plus more sliced for topping

4 fresh sage leaves

¼ teaspoon nutmeg

½ cup brown rice flour

3 cups cooked quinoa

Preheat the oven to 400°F. Place the butternut squash, cut-side up, on one half of a baking sheet and the sliced onions on the other. Drizzle with 1 tablespoon olive oil. Gently toss the onions to make sure they're completely coated with oil. Spread them in a single layer on the baking sheet and bake. After about 30 minutes, just as the onions start to brown, use a spatula to remove them from the baking sheet. Reserve them for later. Bake the squash for another 15 to 25 minutes or until fork-tender (45 to 55 minutes total baking time for the squash). Remove from the oven and allow to cool.

When the squash has cooled to the touch, scoop out the insides. You should have about 1½ cups cooked squash.

Reserve ¼ cup cooked onions for the topping the burgers and put the rest in the blender with the squash, egg, grated Parmesan, sage leaves, nutmeg, and brown rice flour. Pulse several times until thoroughly blended.

Using a spatula, scrape the blender contents into a bowl with the cooked quinoa. Stir the mixture gently together and form into four to six large patties, depending on your preference.

Preheat the oven to 350°F. Heat the remaining tablespoon of oil over medium-high heat in an oven-safe frying pan or cast-iron pan. When the oil is nice and hot, gently slide in the burgers (as many as you can fit comfortably without them crowding one another).

Let the burgers cook for about 6 to 8 minutes on the stove top, flipping them halfway through. Next, with the burgers still in it, place the pan in the oven to bake for another 8 to 10 minutes. Top with the Parmesan slices after about 7 minutes of baking time, and remove from the oven when the cheese is melted. The total cooking time is about 15 minutes.

Top with the reserved oven-roasted onions and serve over a bed of dressed greens.

CHAPTER 10

Main Dishes

Unh-unh, there's no chicken in the blender happening here, I promise. There are a few shrimp that get chopped by the blender blades, though, and some mighty luscious sauces and fillings are blended up. Marinades also play a major role in the main courses in this chapter. The concentrated flavors enhance meats, and the acidity of the marinades makes them more juicy and tender.

All these sauces can be made in advance, and most of them can be frozen. When I make Spinach Chicken Enchiladas and Artichoke Ricotta Manicotti, I often double the recipe, assemble half in a foil pan, and freeze it for another meal. Homemade prepared food. It makes me so happy! After a busy day, I don't have to think about dinner knowing there's a complete one that only needs to be heated.

Another bonus: versatility. Pesto of course is not just for rigatoni, and Spicy Aïoli complements many types of fish. Tikka masala sauce works well with almost any vegetables, and red pepper sauce makes a great pizza crust topper.

Caribbean Shrimp Fritters with Spicy Aïoli

serves 4

I'm a sucker for all things fried. I don't think I've ever turned down a piece of crispy fried calamari or deep-fried chicken. And fritters, oh man. Apple fritters, conch fritters, corn fritters—I eat 'em all. You can only imagine how high up these shrimp fritters—originally a creation of my friend Jenny—are on my list of favorites. They make a scrumptious starter, but also work well as a main course paired with some satiating sides like Asian Slaw (page 194) and Summer Corn and Avocado Salad (page 139).

For the Caribbean Shrimp Fritters

¼ cup chopped onion

1 garlic clove, peeled and cut in half

½ red pepper, seeded and cut into large chunks

1 cup raw shrimp, peeled and tails removed

2 large eggs

1 cup all-purpose flour

1 teaspoon baking powder

1 tablespoon Old Bay seasoning

½ teaspoon black pepper

¼–½ cup water

Peanut oil

For the Spicy Aïoli

1 cup prepared mayonnaise or Basic Aïoli (page 113)

2–3 tablespoons Dijon mustard

2–3 tablespoons lime juice

2 tablespoons raw honey

2–3 teaspoons Old Bay seasoning

To make the Spicy Aïoli: Stir together all the ingredients in a small bowl. Set aside.

To make the fritters: Put the onion, garlic, and red pepper in the blender and pulse several times. Add the shrimp and pulse another one or two times.

In a medium bowl, lightly whisk the eggs. Add the flour, baking powder, Old Bay, pepper, and ¼ cup water to make a smooth batter. Fold in the shrimp mixture. If the mixture is too thick, add a little more water.

Heat several inches of peanut oil in a skillet. Drop tablespoonfuls of the batter into the oil and fry until golden brown, about 3 minutes each side, moving them around so they don't stick to the bottom of the pan. Serve warm with Spicy Aïoli.

Spinach Chicken Enchiladas with Ancho Chile Sauce

serves **4–6**

There are several steps to making this dish. You have to make the sauce, then the filling, and finally assemble the enchiladas. You can always make the sauce a day or two in advance, or even assemble the whole dish a day or two before you're serving it. Each element is important to the whole, and truly worth the effort. This dish is always a crowd-pleaser. Please note, you can purchase a rotisserie chicken to use in this recipe, or refer to Chicken Tortilla Soup (page 122) for how to poach and shred a chicken.

For the Ancho Chile Sauce

3 ancho chile pods (about 1½ ounces), stems removed and seeded

1 tablespoon extra-virgin olive oil

1 large onion, coarsely chopped (about 2 cups)

2 garlic cloves, peeled and sliced

1 (32-ounce) can fire-roasted tomatoes, such as Muir Glen Organic

1 cup chicken broth

2 tablespoons balsamic vinegar

2 teaspoons Worcestershire sauce

1 tablespoon freshly squeezed lime juice

½ teaspoon ground cumin

½ teaspoon dried oregano

½ teaspoon kosher salt

⅛ teaspoon freshly ground black pepper

To make the sauce: Put the chiles in a bowl and cover with boiling water. Let stand for 30 minutes, then drain, reserving both the chiles and the liquid.

Heat the oil in a skillet over medium-high heat and sauté the onion and garlic for 5 to 8 minutes or until softened. Add the tomatoes and softened chiles, and cook another 10 minutes. Stir in the rest of the ingredients, cook another minute or so, and transfer the mixture to the blender along with ½ cup of the reserved chile liquid. Blend until smooth. Set aside.

For the filling

3 cups shredded cooked chicken

1 (10-ounce) package frozen chopped spinach, thawed

1 (15-ounce) can black beans, drained and rinsed

1½ cups shredded sharp cheddar cheese

1 cup fresh or frozen corn kernels

4 ounces canned green chiles

1 tablespoon lime juice

¼ cup fresh cilantro leaves

½ teaspoon kosher salt

⅛ teaspoon freshly ground pepper

For the enchiladas

½ cup shredded sharp cheddar cheese

12 small corn tortillas

To make the filling: In a large bowl, put all the ingredients for the enchilada filling. Add 1 cup of the Ancho Chile Sauce and mix together until well combined.

Preheat the oven to 350°F.

To assemble the enchiladas: Pour 1 cup of the Ancho Chile Sauce in the bottom of a 9 x 13-inch baking dish. Dip a tortilla in the sauce and fill with 3 heaping tablespoons of filling. Roll up and place seam-side down in the baking dish. Repeat with the remaining tortillas. Spoon about 1 additional cup sauce over the top of the enchiladas, top with ½ cup cheddar cheese, and bake for 20 minutes or until warmed through and the cheese topping is melted.

Lemon Tarragon Chicken

serves 4–6

The delicate flavor of the tarragon permeates the chicken when it's marinated in this lemony blend. Instead of grilling the chicken, you can roast it in a 500°F oven for 35 to 40 minutes. After removing the chicken from the marinade (save it for the sauce), blot it with a paper towel and divide it between two roasting pans. Rotate the pans several times while roasting. Finish with the reserved marinade as directed below.

½ cup extra-virgin olive oil

¼ cup tarragon vinegar

½ cup freshly squeezed lemon juice (keep the rinds)

2 garlic cloves, peeled

2 teaspoons Dijon mustard

1 teaspoon kosher salt

½ cup fresh tarragon leaves, firmly packed, plus extra for garnish

1 (4½-pound) whole chicken, cut into pieces

Put all the ingredients except the lemon rinds and chicken together in the blender container and blend for 30 seconds or until smooth.

Place the chicken into a resealable plastic bag with the lemon rinds and pour in the marinade. Seal and marinate for 8 hours, or preferably overnight.

Preheat your grill. Remove the chicken from the marinade (save it for the sauce) and cook it indirectly for 30 minutes (coals or gas are hot on one side of the grill, the chicken is on the other), turning as needed. Move the chicken to direct heat for the last 15 to 20 minutes of cooking time to give it good color. Watch carefully so it doesn't burn.

Meanwhile, bring the leftover marinade to a boil and simmer on low for 6 minutes. Pour over the chicken before serving and garnish with fresh tarragon leaves.

Chicken Tikka Masala

serves **4-6**

This chicken is my go-to dish for entertaining. It's the perfect anchor for an all-out Indian meal: papadum, samosas, saag paneer, vegetable biryani, and of course naan. The juicy, flavorful chicken never fails to get rave reviews.

3 garlic cloves, peeled

2-inch piece gingerroot, peeled and cut into chunks (about ⅓ cup)

½ teaspoon whole black peppercorns

2 tablespoons cashew butter

¾ cup plain yogurt

⅓ cup white wine vinegar

⅓ cup extra-virgin olive oil

3 tablespoons tomato paste

2 tablespoon freshly squeezed lemon juice

3 tablespoons Hungarian paprika

5 teaspoons garam masala

¾ teaspoon ground cumin

¾ teaspoon ground coriander

1 teaspoon kosher salt

2 pounds boneless chicken breast and thighs, cut into 2-inch pieces

For the sauce:

1 cup chopped tomatoes

2 tablespoons tomato paste

½ cup plain yogurt

2 tablespoons butter (optional)

fresh cilantro for garnis

Place all the ingredients (except the chicken) in the blender in the order listed. Run on high until smooth, about 2 minutes. Remove ½ cup marinade and reserve to make the sauce. Transfer the marinade to a gallon-sized resealable plastic bag.

Add the chicken and marinate 8 hours or overnight.

Preheat the broiler. Remove the chicken from the marinade and blot it with paper towels to remove the excess marinade.

Place the chicken in a roasting pan and broil for about 12 minutes, turning the pieces about halfway through the cooking time. While the chicken is roasting, make the sauce. Put the reserved ½ cup marinade in a small pan with the tomatoes and tomato paste. Stir thoroughly and bring to a low boil. Lower the heat and gently simmer for 8 minutes. Just before serving, stir in the yogurt (and butter if you're feeling decadent!). Stir in the broiled chicken pieces and any remaining juices that have accumulated. Heat through. Garnish with fresh cilantro leaves. Serve with rice and naan bread.

Roasted Turkey Breast with Chipotle Sauce

serves 4–6

The ubiquitous chicken breast can get a little dull week after week. I find turkey breast, with its especially flavorful meat, a welcome change at the dinner table. Topping the breast with spicy chipotle sauce certainly leaves no room for boredom.

For the Chipotle Sauce

1 (7-ounce) can chipotle peppers
2 teaspoons ground cumin
3 garlic cloves, peeled
3 tablespoons extra-virgin olive oil
3 tablespoons red wine vinegar
1 teaspoon Worcestershire sauce

For the turkey breast

1 (3- to 5-pound) bone-in turkey breast
¼ cup buttermilk
¼ cup water
1 avocado, pitted and peeled
½ teaspoon kosher salt
⅛ teaspoon freshly ground black pepper

To make the Chipotle Sauce: Place all the ingredients in the blender container and run on high until smooth, scraping down the sides of the blender as needed. Scrape all the sauce into a gallon-sized resealable plastic bag, reserving 3 tablespoons for the serving sauce.

To make the turkey breast: Using a sharp knife, make small slits in the turkey breast. Place it in the prepared resealable plastic bag. Seal and marinate for at least 6 hours.

Meanwhile, place the 3 tablespoons reserved Chipotle Sauce (or less if you prefer a milder sauce) in the blender with the buttermilk, water, avocado, and seasonings. Process until smooth. Refrigerate until you're ready to use it.

When the turkey is finished marinating, preheat the oven to 375°F. Blot the marinade off the turkey and place it in a roasting pan. Cook for 1½ to 2 hours or until the internal temperature reaches 165 to 170°F. Allow to rest for 10 minutes before carving. Serve with the prepared Chipotle Sauce.

Sliced Skirt Steak with Chimichurri Sauce

serves 4

Skirt steak is the cut of meat fajitas are made from. Long and thin, the steak, from the diaphragm of a steer, has a very visible loose grain. Serve the flavorful steak with chimichurri sauce. A little salsa-esque, a little pesto-like, the sauce originated in Argentina and is traditionally served as an accompaniment to grilled meats.

2 pounds choice- or prime-grade skirt steak

2 garlic cloves, peeled

½ cup red wine vinegar

Juice of 1 lemon

½ teaspoon salt

1 tablespoon fresh oregano

¾ cup fresh cilantro

½ cup fresh flat-leaf parsley

½ teaspoon dried chili flakes

⅔ cup extra-virgin olive oil

Sea salt and pepper, for seasoning

Pound the meat evenly with a meat mallet and set it aside at room temperature for at least 15 minutes (preferably 30) while you make the sauce.

Place the garlic, vinegar, lemon juice, and salt in the blender jar and run on medium for 2 minutes. Add the oregano, cilantro, parsley, and chili flakes; run on medium for 20 to 30 seconds or until the herbs are chopped and well combined but some texture remains. Use a spatula to scrape the ingredients down from the sides as necessary. Empty the contents of the blender into a small bowl and stir in the olive oil. Set aside.

Season the meat generously with salt and pepper. Grill the steak outdoors over coal or indoors in a grill pan over high heat for about 3 to 4 minutes per side or until your desired doneness is achieved. When the steak is finished cooking, tent it with foil and allow it to rest for 5 minutes. Slice the steak against the grain and spoon a couple of tablespoons of sauce over it, serving the remainder for those who want extra.

Marinated Pork Tenderloin with Cranberry Relish

serves 4

There are fringe benefits to this meal: leftovers. The tender morsels of marinated meat make a darn good pressed sandwich. My husband likes to layer the pork with sliced Swiss cheese (or cheddar), perhaps some sautéed onions, and a spoonful of cranberry relish between two slices of crisp ciabatta. He then presses them in a panini maker, or sometimes opts for the skillet, pressing the sandwich with a smaller heavy pan on top. There are so many options—you could add avocado, pickles, Monterey Jack, coleslaw. Have fun, be inventive.

For the marinade

2 garlic cloves, peeled and cut in half

2 tablespoons fresh rosemary

1 tablespoon raw honey

1 tablespoon Dijon mustard

½ cup freshly squeezed orange juice

Zest of 1 orange

¼ cup extra-virgin olive oil

For the pork

2 pork tenderloins, about 1 pound each

Kosher salt and freshly ground black pepper

2 tablespoons extra-virgin olive oil

To make the marinade: Put all the ingredients in the blender and process on high for 60 seconds or until the mixture is thoroughly combined.

To marinate the pork: Using a knife, make small slits in the pork tenderloins and place them in a resealable plastic bag. Add the marinade and refrigerate for at least 4 hours or overnight.

1¼ cups fresh or frozen cranberries

½ orange, seeds removed and cut into quarters

¼ cup freshly squeezed orange juice

¼ cup maple syrup

1 garlic clove, peeled

1 tablespoon fresh rosemary, plus extra sprig or two for garnish

2 teaspoons extra-virgin olive oil

To make the relish: Combine all the ingredients (except the oil) in the blender jar and pulse until just combined. You want to maintain some texture and not turn the mixture into a paste. Next, heat the 2 teaspoons olive oil in a small pan over medium heat. Add the relish and cook for 10 minutes to meld the flavors. Set aside.

Preheat the oven to 400°F. Remove the tenderloins from the marinade and blot dry. Generously salt and pepper the tenderloins. Heat the 2 tablespoons olive oil in an ovenproof sauté pan or cast-iron skillet over medium-high heat. Sear the pork tenderloins on all sides until golden brown.

Transfer the skillet or pan to the preheated oven and roast the tenderloins for about 12 to 15 minutes or until a meat thermometer reads 140°F. Remove the pork from the oven, tent with foil, and let it stand for about 10 minutes.

To serve, cut the pork in ½-inch slices, place the slices on a plate, drizzle any juices from the pan over them, and garnish with the cranberry relish and rosemary sprigs, if desired.

Spinach Pesto Sauce with Rigatoni

By no means should your use of this pesto be limited to pasta. Spread it on panini, put it in a quiche, or add it to a dip. You can also play around with the ingredients. Substitute kale for the spinach or try Romano cheese instead of Parm. And again, go easy with the blending so you preserve some texture in the sauce.

¼ cup pine nuts or walnuts

2½ ounces Parmesan cheese

1 garlic clove, peeled

2 cups fresh basil leaves, washed and patted dry

2 cups fresh spinach leaves, stems removed

⅔ cup extra-virgin olive oil

½ teaspoon kosher salt

1 pound dried rigatoni

1 pint cherry tomatoes, cut in half

½ pound fresh mozzarella, cut into ½-inch cubes

Put the nuts in a skillet and cook on the stovetop over medium-high heat, stirring constantly, for about 4 to 6 minutes. Set aside to cool.

Meanwhile, put the Parmesan and the garlic in the blender and pulse. Add the pine nuts and pulse two more times.

Add the basil, spinach, oil, and salt. Pulse until just blended.

Cook the rigatoni according to the package directions and drain. Return the cooked pasta to the pot, add the tomatoes, and toss immediately with the Spinach Pesto. Stir in the fresh mozzarella. Serve warm or at room temperature.

Artichoke Ricotta Manicotti with Sneak-It-In Veggie Sauce

serves 4–6

Much like the Spinach Chicken Enchiladas with Ancho Chile Sauce, this dish takes several steps to assemble. If you make the sauce in big batches, though, you can have it on hand to complete this dish. It freezes really well.

This exceptionally palatable sauce is chock-full of vegetables. While I prefer to embrace the idea of healthy eating, and teach kids (and adults alike!) to love veggies, sometimes they just won't bend and refuse to eat what's good for them. Enter this stealth Sneak-It-In Veggie Sauce. The creamy reddish-orange sauce really looks no different from tomato sauce, but you and I will know the punch it packs.

1 large egg

1 (24-ounce) container ricotta cheese (about 2⅔ cups)

⅔ cup freshly grated Parmesan cheese, divided

1 teaspoon dried oregano

½ teaspoon kosher salt

⅛ teaspoon freshly ground pepper, or to taste

¼ teaspoon freshly grated nutmeg

1 (14-ounce) can water-packed artichoke hearts, drained

1½ cups packed baby spinach leaves (about 2 ounces)

10 cooked manicotti shells

3 cups Sneak-It-In Veggie Sauce (recipe follows)

Fresh basil leaves, for garnish

Preheat the oven to 350°F. Put the egg, ricotta, ⅓ cup of the Parmesan cheese, oregano, salt, pepper, and nutmeg in the blender and run for 10 seconds on high.

Add the artichoke hearts and spinach leaves to the blender and pulse several times until incorporated.

Using a spatula, scrape the mixture into a large resealable plastic bag. Cut off one corner of the bag and squeeze the filling into the cooked manicotti shells.

Spread 1 cup of the sauce into the bottom of a 9 x 13-inch baking dish. Place the filled manicotti shells in the dish, cover with another cup of sauce, and sprinkle with the reserved ⅓ cup grated Parmesan cheese.

Bake for 30 minutes or until heated through. Garnish with fresh basil leaves and serve.

makes 3 cups sauce

Sneak-It-In Veggie Sauce

¼ cup extra-virgin olive oil

1 garlic clove, peeled and sliced

1 small onion, sliced

2 carrots, peeled and cut into 1-inch chunks

1 red or orange bell pepper, seeded and cut into chunks

1 small zucchini, cut into small chunks

1 (28-ounce) can fire-roasted tomatoes

1 bay leaf

1 teaspoon kosher salt

⅛ teaspoon freshly ground pepper

Heat the olive oil in a skillet over medium-high heat. Add the garlic, onion, carrots, pepper, and zucchini to the pan. Sauté for 8 to 10 minutes, or until the vegetables are softened.

Add the tomatoes, bay leaf, salt, and pepper; reduce the heat and simmer for another 10 minutes.

Remove the pan from the heat, remove the bay leaf, and transfer the sauce to the blender jar using a ladle. Run for 10 to 15 seconds on high or until the sauce is nearly smooth. Use for Artichoke Ricotta Manicotti.

Vietnamese-Style Summer Rolls with Peanut Dipping Sauce

makes **8 rolls**

Light and refreshing, these rolls are perfect for a picnic (if you transport them or don't eat them immediately, wrap them in a damp paper towel to keep them from drying out) or a healthy dinner. Once you've prepped all the ingredients, the assembly moves along quite fast, but it does take some practice. The rice wrappers are delicate, and can tear easily. Give yourself a few trial runs. Add some other fillings, too: avocado, shrimp, chicken, scallions. The pairing of crunchy salad ingredients with soft noodles creates an interesting contrast of flavors and textures. And don't forget the peanut sauce: It's the icing on the cake.

3 ounces dried rice vermicelli

¼ cup freshly squeezed lime juice, divided

1 teaspoon organic cane sugar

1 medium cucumber, seeded and cut into 4-inch-long matchsticks

3 small carrots, shredded (about 1 cup)

8 (8½-inch) round rice paper wrappers

Red lettuce leaves, cut in quarters

½ cup loosely packed fresh mint leaves

½ cup loosely packed fresh cilantro sprigs

½ cup crushed peanuts

1 tablespoon finely minced jalapeño

Cook the noodles according the directions on the package and toss with 2 tablespoons of the lime juice after draining. Set aside.

Mix together the remaining 2 tablespoons lime juice with the sugar and sprinkle half over the cucumber and half over the carrots, tossing lightly.

Have all your ingredients for filling the rolls set out and ready.

Spread a damp kitchen towel on the counter. Fill a pie pan with warm tap water. Completely submerge a rice wrapper in the water and place it on the towel.

Working quickly while the wrapper is pliable, lay a handful of noodles (about ⅓ to ½ cup) on the wrapper, then place one piece of lettuce, six cucumber sticks, 1 heaping tablespoon of carrots, several mint and cilantro leaves, and about 1 tablespoon peanuts on or next to the noodles.

Wet your fingers and pull the bottom of the wrapper up over the fillings. Next, pull the left side of the wrapper up and over the fillings and keep it taut as you roll the wrapper tightly toward you. Repeat with all the wrappers. Cut the rolls and serve with Peanut Dipping Sauce.

Peanut Dipping Sauce

makes 1 cup

½ cup smooth peanut butter
2 tablespoons soy sauce
2 tablespoons sesame oil
2 tablespoons rice wine vinegar
1 garlic clove, peeled
½-inch piece gingerroot, peeled
1 tablespoon lime juice
6 tablespoons water

Place everything in the blender and process on high for 20 seconds until smooth.

CHAPTER 11

Vegetables

You can use the blender to camouflage veggies in your diet, but you can also use it to play up those beauties. While pureeing vegetables may seem like a no-brainer, it does actually take some thought. Adding some type of fat and spices helps add richness, and roasting or sautéing those luscious edibles heightens flavors.

Highlight veggies as a main course. Fill your plate with two purees and add a salad for texture, or serve Asian Slaw and Crispy Zucchini Fries with a veggie burger. Veggies can also greatly enhance a meat dish: Indian Spiced Spinach is an excellent accompaniment to Chicken Tikka Masala (page 173) and Creamy Cauliflower Mash perfectly complements Marinated Pork Tenderloin with Cranberry Relish (page 176).

Vegetables are so good for you that it's really hard to eat too many, as long as you prepare them healthfully (no smothering in heavy cheese sauces!). They are low in calories and sugar and high in vitamins and fiber. They are also rich in phytonutrients—active compounds that have been shown to lower the risk of disease, more specifically termed antioxidants, flavonoids, and carotenoids, among others. Hundreds of phytonutrients have been classified, and it's this variety that gives vegetables their different colors. Eating a wide array of types and colors of vegetables helps ensure you obtain a beneficial level of phytonutrients in your diet. Just like Mama said, "Eat your veggies!"

French Green Beans with Walnut Miso Butter

serves 4

Don't reserve Walnut Miso Butter strictly for beans. Try it slathered on carrots or tossed with broccoli or even mixed with a mélange of steamed veggies.

¾ cup plus 2 tablespoons walnuts
1 garlic clove, peeled
2 tablespoons sesame oil
1 tablespoon rice wine vinegar
1 tablespoon water
2 teaspoons raw honey
3 tablespoons white miso paste
1 pound French green beans

Toast the walnuts: Put the walnuts in a dry skillet over medium-high heat on the stove top for 4 to 5 minutes stirring frequently until they become fragrant. Remove from the skillet and cool before blending. Place ¾ cup toasted walnuts and the garlic clove in the blender pitcher. Pulse several times on medium. Using a spatula, scrape down the sides of the blender and pulse again.

Add the sesame oil, vinegar, water, raw honey, and miso paste. Process for 30 seconds or until blended thoroughly. Set aside.

Heat an inch or so of water in a skillet and bring it to a boil. Add the string beans and cook for 3 to 4 minutes. Quickly drain and place back in the pan. Toss with the miso butter then transfer the beans to a serving dish. Coarsely chop the remaining 2 tablespoons walnuts and sprinkle on the beans. Serve warm.

Baked Eggplant Puree

serves 4–6

This dish is the perfect accompaniment for roasted meats or pasta tossed with a rich tomato sauce. Leftover eggplant puree also makes a delicious pasta sauce itself! Simply heat it and toss with penne. Perhaps throw in some cherry tomatoes, too.

3 eggplants (about 3 pounds total)
3 unpeeled garlic cloves
1 tablespoon extra-virgin olive oil
1 tablespoon freshly squeezed lemon juice
½ teaspoon kosher salt

For the topping

1 garlic clove, peeled
¼ cup whole wheat bread crumbs
¼ cup feta cheese
1 teaspoon extra-virgin olive oil

Preheat the oven to 400°F. Cut the eggplants in half and place them on a foil-lined baking sheet with the unpeeled garlic cloves; set the sheet in the oven to roast. After 30 minutes, take out the eggplant, but let the garlic continue to roast for another 15 minutes.

In the meantime, scoop out the inside of the eggplant and drain in a colander for 15 minutes.

To make the topping: Put the raw garlic clove in the blender and process for 10 seconds. Add the bread crumbs, feta, and olive oil to the blender, and pulse four times. Remove from the blender and set aside.

Reduce the oven to 375°F. Squeeze the roasted garlic out of the peels. When the eggplant is drained, place it in the blender with the roasted garlic, olive oil, lemon juice, and salt. Pulse several times.

Pour the mixture into an 8-inch-square baking dish, and sprinkle with the bread crumb mixture. Bake for 15 minutes or until the topping is bubbling. Serve warm.

Herbed Carrot-Parsnip Puree

There's something very satisfying about this sweet and creamy dish, which makes it a year-round favorite. The bright orange puree is light enough to serve in summer, yet is also nourishing enough to be comforting in winter.

1½ pounds carrots (about 9 medium), peeled and cut into 2-inch chunks

¾ pound parsnips (about 3), peeled and cut into 2-inch chunks

1 garlic clove, peeled

¼ cup coconut milk

5 teaspoons extra-virgin olive oil

2 teaspoons fresh thyme

Place the carrots, parsnips, and garlic in a 2-quart pot filled three-quarters with water. Bring the water to a boil, then turn the heat down and simmer the carrots and parsnips for about 15 minutes or until the vegetables are fork-tender.

When the vegetables are done cooking, drain them and put them in the blender container with the rest of the ingredients. Process for about 30 seconds on medium or until the mixture becomes creamy and smooth. Serve immediately.

Asian Slaw

The texture of shredded coleslaw is a nice complement to many main courses, especially grilled fish and chicken. For a more traditional slaw, mix shredded cabbage with Basic Aïoli (page 113). This recipe uses a water chopping method that quickly dices large amounts of vegetables. However, it is very important that you drain the vegetables completely or you'll end up with a watery mess. Use extra paper towels if necessary to absorb the excess water.

½ head cabbage, cored and cut into quarters

2 carrots, peeled and cut into 2-inch chunks

1 whole scallion, trimmed and cut into 2-inch chunks

1 tablespoon soy sauce

1 tablespoon lime juice

1 tablespoon sesame oil

2 tablespoons rice wine vinegar

2 teaspoons dark brown sugar

½-inch piece fresh gingerroot, peeled

1 garlic clove, peeled

1 tablespoon water

Put the cabbage in the blender and cover with water. Pulse four or five times or until finely chopped. Drain in a fine-mesh sieve and put into a paper-towel-lined bowl. Place a doubled paper towel on top of the cabbage. Repeat the blender-water chopping with the carrots and scallion at the same time. Drain the mixture in the sieve and put it on top of the paper towel.

Put all the remaining ingredients in the cleaned blender jar and process on high until smooth.

Remove the paper towel from the bowl and toss the slaw with the dressing. Refrigerate until you're ready to serve.

Crispy Zucchini Fries

serves 4

I'm going to be completely up front here: These take more time than you may think. It takes some dipping and coating to produce perfectly crunchy-on-the-outside, tender-on-the-inside zucchini sticks, but the end result is well worth the investment. If you're short on time, you can always use store-bought panko. This breading method can be applied to many foods, including shrimp, chicken cutlets, eggplant, and a multitude of other vegetables. You can shallow-fry the items for an even crispier coating.

6 pieces firm whole wheat bread

3–4 large eggs

½ cup all-purpose flour

¾ teaspoon kosher salt

¼ teaspoon freshly ground black pepper

½ cup Parmesan cheese

2 zucchini (about ¾ pound), cut into 4-inch french-fry-like strips

Preheat the oven to 400°F and line two baking sheets with parchment paper.

Remove the crusts from the bread and tear each slice into several pieces as you put it in the blender. Pulse the blender two or three times, until the bread resembles coarse panko-like bread crumbs.

Spread the bread crumbs in a thin layer on one of the parchment-lined baking sheets. Bake them for 6 to 8 minutes or until they are thoroughly dried, but not browned.

When the bread crumbs are finished baking, set them aside to cool for a few minutes. Meanwhile, put the eggs in a shallow dish and lightly beat them. In another shallow dish, mix the flour, salt, and pepper. Lastly, put the cooled bread crumbs (you should have about 1½ cups) in a third dish (or pile them on a piece of waxed paper) and with your hands, gently mix in the Parmesan cheese.

Working in batches, dip each zucchini strip first in the flour, then the egg, then finally the bread crumb mixture. Arrange the strips in a single layer on the two prepared pans (you can reuse the parchment you baked the bread crumbs on). Bake the fries for 20 to 25 minutes, turning once during the baking time to ensure that they are golden and crispy on all sides.

Serve with Basic Aïoli (page 113).

Indian Spiced Spinach

serves **4–6**

The fusion of flavors in this dish was inspired by Myra Kornfeld, a chef, teacher, writer, and—most important—coconut genius! Coconut milk subtly marries the spinach and spices, creating a harmonious dish that will be gone before you can reach for seconds. My daughter believes that it's so good, she says it's like dessert—and in my experience, not many spinach dishes garner that reaction.

1-inch piece peeled gingerroot

1 small onion, peeled and cut into quarters

1 garlic clove, peeled and cut in half

1 teaspoon ground cumin

1 teaspoon garam masala

½ teaspoon kosher salt

2 tablespoons water

3 tablespoons coconut oil, divided

1 shallot, peeled and sliced into thin rings

1 tablespoon coconut flour or all-purpose flour

1 (11-ounce) container baby spinach (about 8 packed cups)

½ cup coconut milk

Freshly ground black pepper to taste

Put the ginger, onion, garlic, cumin, garam masala, salt, and water in the blender. Process on medium for about 20 seconds, until the mixture forms a smooth paste. Use a spatula to scrape the sides and push the ingredients toward the blade and process longer if necessary.

Heat 1 tablespoon of the coconut oil in a large Dutch oven over medium-high heat. Meanwhile, dredge the sliced shallot rings in the flour and gently slide them into the hot oil. Stir them lightly until they're golden and crispy. Using a spoon, transfer them to a plate lined with a paper towel to drain.

Heat the remaining oil in the Dutch oven over medium heat. Add the spice paste and sauté for about 1 minute. Add the spinach, toss it with the paste, and cook until everything is thoroughly combined.

Pour in the coconut milk and stir well. Bring the milk to a simmer, then reduce the heat and cook on low for about 4 minutes. Season with pepper to taste, and more salt if needed. Transfer to a serving dish and top with fried shallots.

Vegetables

197

Creamy Cauliflower Mash

serves 4

This low-carb alternative to mashed potatoes is so silky and smooth that you may find you like it better than traditional spuds, which can turn out lumpy, bumpy, and gluey. Just make sure you drain the cauliflower really well after boiling it, perhaps even placing it on a paper towel for a few minutes before pureeing to prevent a watery texture.

1 head cauliflower, cleaned, cored, and cut into florets

1 garlic clove, peeled

1 tablespoon cream cheese

2 tablespoons grated Parmesan cheese

3 tablespoons milk

½ teaspoon kosher salt

Freshly ground black pepper to taste

Bring a large pot of water to a boil. Add the cauliflower florets and garlic clove. Bring the water back to a boil then reduce the heat to medium-low and simmer for 8 minutes.

After 8 minutes, check that the cauliflower is fork-tender. If not, continue to cook until it is. Drain well.

Add the drained cauliflower, garlic clove, cheeses, milk, and salt to the blender pitcher. Run on medium for 30 seconds, using a spatula to scrape down the sides of the pitcher as necessary.

Pour the mash into a serving bowl. Add black pepper to taste and stir well.

Fresh Corn Cakes

makes **12–15 cakes**

These gluten-free corn cakes are not to be confused with corn fritters. They're flatter, more like pancakes. The binders here are fresh-ground cornmeal (page 43), eggs, and ricotta. The cornmeal does give these cakes some texture. If you prefer a finer consistency, replace all or half the cornmeal with all-purpose flour. Either way, the focus is truly on the corn.

2 trimmed scallions, white parts only

1 jalapeño, seeded and cut into quarters

2 large eggs

½ cup ricotta cheese

½ teaspoon kosher salt

¼ cup finely ground cornmeal

1½ cups fresh corn cut from the cob, or frozen corn kernels

¼ cup crumbled goat cheese or grated cheddar cheese

2 tablespoons unsalted butter

Sour cream and freshly cut chives, for garnish

Place the scallions and jalapeño in the blender and process on medium for 10 seconds. Scrape down the sides of the blender, pushing the ingredients toward the blade, and pulse again.

Add the eggs, ricotta, and salt. Process again on medium another 10 seconds.

Finally, add the cornmeal and pulse until combined.

Put the mixture into a small bowl and stir in the corn and cheese.

Heat 1 tablespoon of the butter in a skillet or fry pan over medium heat. Using a tablespoon measure, scoop out heaping spoonfuls of batter onto the pan, making about 3-inch diameter cakes. Fry them for about 2 minutes on each side. Try not to flip them prematurely as they'll fall apart. Carefully lift the edge of one cake with a spatula to see if it's ready to flip. After the first batch is done, add the second tablespoon of butter to the pan and repeat with the remaining batter.

Serve warm with sour cream and chives as garnish.

Roasted Root Veggies with Romesco Sauce

serves 6   *Romesco is a garlicky sauce that originated in Spain. I've encountered quite a few variations on this mild sauce over the years, and seen it used in many ways— over vegetables, with fish, and even with a salad. Here I've paired it with roasted vegetables, but it's even good just spread on a piece of warm baguette.*

1 ancho chile, cored and seeded

3 red peppers, seeded and cut in half lengthwise, or 1 (24-ounce) jar roasted peppers

⅓ cup hazelnuts, skinned (page 85)

1 (14-ounce) can fire-roasted tomatoes, such as Muir Glen

3 garlic cloves, peeled

2 tablespoons flat-leaf parsley, plus extra for garnish

2 tablespoons red wine vinegar

1 teaspoon smoked paprika

¼ cup plus 2 tablespoons extra-virgin olive oil

3-pound assortment of root vegetables (such as carrots, parsnips, purple and white potatoes, and sweet potatoes), peeled and cut into 2-inch cubes

½ teaspoon kosher salt

¼ teaspoon freshly ground black pepper

Preheat the oven to 450°F. Place the ancho chile in a bowl and cover it with boiling water. Allow it to sit for 30 minutes, then drain.

Place the red peppers on a foil-lined baking sheet and set in the oven for 40 minutes or until the skins have begun to char and are wrinkled. Then remove the peppers from the oven and immediately put them in a brown paper bag to steam. Make sure the top of the bag is tightly rolled down to create a seal. After about 15 minutes, the peppers should be cool enough to handle and you will be able to easily remove the skins. Reduce the oven temperature to 400°F.

Meanwhile, put the hazelnuts in the blender and pulse them until they're coarsely ground. When your peppers are ready, add them to the blender with the reserved chile, tomatoes, garlic, parsley, vinegar, paprika, and ¼ cup of the oil. Puree until smooth.

Put the cubed vegetables on a baking sheet and toss with the remaining 2 tablespoons olive oil and the salt and pepper. Roast for 40 minutes or until tender and golden, turning the vegetables several times with a spatula while roasting.

Transfer the roasted vegetables to a bowl and toss with Romesco Sauce. Garnish with chopped parsley and serve.

CHAPTER 12

Desserts

When a friend of mine recently bought a blender, she bragged, "We're eating dessert every night! And it's healthy!" But isn't that an oxymoron? Healthy dessert? Well, this is the beauty of the blender: the sneak-it-in factor. With the blender you can add healthy fats like avocado to chocolate mousse for texture and black beans to brownies for fiber and protein—without anyone detecting it. In fact, sometimes it seems better kept a secret. The idea of beans in brownies does not exactly conjure up visions of a bakery-like confection, but I swear it tastes like one.

My friend, on the other hand, uses the blender to make healthy "soft ice cream" as she likes to call it. She blends up frozen fruit to make a sorbet-like dessert. Try it with your favorite fruit. The blender is also good for mixing up crusts. While the desserts here do contain sugar, I've kept the amounts low, and there are numerous gluten-free options. While desserts will never replace the goodness value of vegetables, you can always make them better with the blender.

Lime Tartlets with Coconut Crusts

makes **24 tartlets**

The coconut crusts of these tartlets are a dessert in themselves. My daughter Anna likes to eat them empty. She also likes them filled with chocolate ganache. The creamy mascarpone filling is just one of many that you can use to fill these sweet crusts. A scoop of lemon curd would do quite nicely, or perhaps even a small scoop of ice cream.

2¾ cups sweetened coconut

3 large egg whites

1 teaspoon pure vanilla extract

Pinch of kosher salt

1 (8-ounce) container mascarpone cheese

3 tablespoons raw honey

1 teaspoon grated lime zest, plus more for garnish

Finely diced pineapple and papaya, whole black raspberries, or other favorite fruits, for topping

Preheat the oven to 350°F. Grease a mini muffin pan with baking spray. Put the coconut, egg whites, vanilla, and salt in the blender and run on medium for 1 minute or until throughly combined. Use a spatula to push the ingredients toward the blade if necessary. or until thoroughly combined. Put about 1 tablespoon of the mixture in each muffin cup; press down each one with a tart tamper, or make a small depression using your fingers. Put the pan in the oven and bake for 15 minutes, or until the crusts are just beginning to brown. Remove the crusts from the pan very soon after you take the pan out of the oven so they don't begin to stick.

Next, whip the mascarpone cheese, honey, and lime zest in the blender until creamy. Fill each shell with a spoonful of the mascarpone mixture and top with a tiny amount of fruit. When all the tarts are filled and topped, sprinkle with lime zest. Chill until ready to serve.

Tart Lemon Squares

These lemon bars have tang! The crust is dense and thick and is an equal partner to the citrusy, curd-like topping that's tart, but not too much so. The base stays somewhat soft, but doesn't turn soggy either, which makes these bars easy to bite into. When life gives you lemons, make lemon bars.

¾ cup old-fashioned rolled oats
¾ cup white whole wheat flour
¼ cup almond flour
¼ cup maple syrup
¼ cup coconut oil, melted

For the filling

4 large eggs plus 2 egg yolks
½ cup freshly squeezed lemon juice
¾ cup organic cane sugar
1 tablespoon lemon zest
1 teaspoon pure vanilla extract
⅓ cup almond flour
Confectioners' sugar, for dusting

Preheat the oven to 350°F. Grease an 8 x 8-inch baking pan with baking spray. Blend the oats and two flours on medium-high for 20 seconds. Add the rest of the crust ingredients and run on medium for 20 seconds. Press into the prepared pan and bake for 15 minutes.

To make the filling: Put all the filling ingredients (except the confectioners' sugar) in the blender container and beat on low for 15 seconds. Do not over-process or the mixture will become too aerated.

Pour the mixture into the prepared crust and bake for another 25 minutes or until the filling is set. Using a fine sieve, dust the top with confectioners' sugar.

Fudgy Gluten-Free Brownies

makes 1 (9-inch) pan

If you think it's sneaky to add peppers and zucchini to a pasta sauce (page 181), how about putting black beans in brownies? I know it may sound unappetizing, but it's one of those "you have to try it to believe it" scenarios. These gluten-free brownies, with the added benefit of fiber and protein, are almost too good to be true. Go ahead, give 'em a try.

8 dates, pitted
½ cup boiling water
1 15-ounce can black beans, drained
½ cup unsweetened cocoa powder
½ cup oat flour
2 large eggs
¼ cup coconut oil
¼ teaspoon kosher salt
1 tablespoon pure vanilla extract
⅓ cup brown rice syrup
1 teaspoon baking powder
1 teaspoon instant espresso powder
¾ cup bittersweet chocolate baking chips or chunks

Put the dates in a small bowl and cover with boiling water. Set aside to soak for 10 minutes. Preheat the oven to 350°F. Grease a 9 x 9-inch baking pan with baking spray and line it with parchment paper, leaving a 1-inch overhang on two sides.

Drain the dates and add to the blender jar with all the ingredients except for the chocolate chunks and process on high for up to $2\frac{1}{2}$ minutes, or until the mixture is smooth.

Using a spatula, stir $\frac{1}{2}$ cup of the chocolate chunks into the mixture in the blender. Pour the batter into the prepared pan and spread evenly. Sprinkle the remaining $\frac{1}{4}$ cup chocolate chunks on top of the brownies.

Bake for 20 to 25 minutes or until a toothpick inserted into the brownies comes out clean of batter (it may have melted chocolate from a chip on it, but you'll recognize the difference—the melted chocolate is thicker and smoother).

Allow to cool and remove the brownies from the pan using the parchment to lift them. Cut into squares and serve.

Wholesome Chocolate Mousse

serves 6

Another covert dessert, this creamy mousse features a base of avocados for a good dose of potassium and fiber. Not what you'd expect from a rich chocolaty treat.

5 dates, pitted
½ cup boiling water
¼ cup chocolate chips
¼ cup almond milk
2 ripe avocados, pitted and peeled
½ cup unsweetened cocoa powder
2 tablespoons maple syrup
1 teaspoon instant coffee
2 teaspoons pure vanilla extract
Pinch of kosher salt

Put the dates in a small bowl and cover with boiling water. Set aside to soak for 10 minutes. Meanwhile melt the chocolate chips in a double boiler. Stir until completely melted. Set aside to cool.

After the dates have soaked, drain them and put them in the blender and pulse several times. Add the almond milk, avocados, cocoa powder, maple syrup, coffee, vanilla, salt, and cooled chocolate chips. Blend until smooth.

Spoon the mixture into small 4-ounce ramekins and chill for at least 2 hours.

Blueberry Cheesecake Bites

makes **30 bites**

Instead of making a traditional cheesecake crust using graham crackers, I like to use oaty British digestive biscuits, such as HobNobs. Many types of cookies will work, though—chocolate wafers, gingersnaps, and plain butter cookies. Weetabix cereal biscuits are another grainy option.

1½ cups cookie crumbs, such as HobNobs (or graham crackers)

¼ cup (½ stick) unsalted butter, melted

3 large eggs

1½ cups cream cheese, softened (12 ounces)

¾ cup ricotta cheese

1 teaspoon pure vanilla extract

2 teaspoons orange zest

½ cup organic cane sugar

Preheat the oven to 350°F. Grease a mini-muffin pan and set aside. Put the cookie crumbs and butter in the blender and process until combined. Using a teaspoon measure, put a spoonful in the bottom of each muffin cup and press the mixture down (you do not need to push it up the sides). Bake for 10 minutes or until lightly browned.

Reduce the oven temperature to 325°F. Meanwhile, mix together the remaining ingredients in the blender container and process for 20 seconds or until combined.

Fill each muffin cup almost to the top and bake for 25 minutes. Top each bite with ½ teaspoon Simple Blueberry Sauce (below).

Simple Blueberry Sauce

2 cups blueberries

3 tablespoons organic cane sugar

1 tablespoon freshly squeezed orange juice

Bring all the ingredients to a boil, reduce the heat, and simmer for 10 minutes. Let the sauce cool—it will thicken as it does so. Use to top Blueberry Cheesecake Bites.

Gluten-Free Raspberry Swirl Cupcakes

makes **18 cupcakes**

I swear, you wouldn't know these cupcakes are gluten-free if I hadn't told you (although I guess you'd figure it out by the ingredients list). They are dense, moist, and not too sweet. The addition of pureed raspberry gives a zip that is complemented by the sweet cream cheese frosting. Even non gluten-free folks should give these a whirl! And note, while there's only $\frac{1}{2}$ teaspoon xanthan gum in the recipe, please don't exclude it or you may not be happy with the end result.

2 cups raspberries

¾ cup plus 1 tablespoon organic cane sugar

3 ounces white chocolate

6 large eggs

¼ cup buttermilk

4-inch piece vanilla bean, seeds scraped out

1 teaspoon pure vanilla extract

½ cup aroma-free coconut oil, melted, or canola oil

¾ cup coconut flour

½ cup white rice flour

½ teaspoon xanthan gum

½ teaspoon kosher salt

1 teaspoon baking powder

Preheat the oven to 325°F. Line a 12-cup muffin tin with paper liners.

Put the raspberries in the blender and puree on high for 1 minute. Push the raspberries through a fine-mesh strainer to remove the seeds. Stir in 1 tablespoon of the sugar and set aside.

Next, melt the white chocolate over a double boiler and whisk until smooth. Set aside to cool.

Put the eggs, remaining ¾ cup sugar, buttermilk, vanilla bean and extract, and oil into the blender. Run on medium for 10 seconds or until blended.

Add the melted chocolate and pulse a few more times until it's fully incorporated.

Finally, add the flours, xanthan gum, salt, and baking powder. Pulse again until just combined.

Fill each liner about three-quarters full. Using a teaspoon measure, put 1 to 2 teaspoons of raspberry puree in the center of each cupcake and, with a toothpick, swirl it clockwise into the batter to create a marbled effect. The batter will be somewhat thick, so just swirl as best you can. Bake for 20 minutes or until the cupcakes are golden. Frost with Raspberry Cream Cheese Frosting (below).

Raspberry Cream Cheese Frosting

makes 2 cups

6 tablespoons unsalted butter, at room temperature

3 ounces cream cheese, at room temperature

4 cups confectioners' sugar

⅓ cup fresh raspberries (about 2 ounces)

Put all the ingredients in the blender and process on medium for 20 seconds, then scrape down the sides using a spatula and repeat the process, continuing to process and scrape until the mixture is light and fluffy. You will probably process for a total of 1 to 1½ minutes. Be careful not to overprocess or the frosting will become runny. Use to frost Raspberry Swirl Cupcakes.

Chai Tea Cake

serves 12

An infusion of aromatic spiced black tea gives this cake a subtle hint of cinnamon, cardamom, ginger, and clove. The moist, fragrant cake keeps well, and can be made a day or two in advance. The creamy frosting, also infused with chai tea, ensures every bite is flavorful.

1 cup (2 sticks) unsalted butter

2 tablespoons chai tea (about 6–7 tea bags)

3 large eggs, at room temperature

1¾ cups organic cane sugar

½ cup firmly packed light brown sugar

2¼ cups all-purpose flour

1½ teaspoons baking powder

½ teaspoon kosher salt

¾ cup buttermilk

½ teaspoon pure vanilla extract

For the glaze

1 cup firmly packed light brown sugar

¼ cup buttermilk

2 tablespoons unsalted butter

1 tablespoon chai tea

Preheat the oven to 350°F. Place the butter in a small saucepan and cook over medium-high heat until completely melted. Add the tea to the butter, reduce the heat, and simmer for 1 minute, stirring occasionally, then turn off the heat and allow the tea to steep in the butter for another 5 minutes.

After the tea has steeped, pour it through a fine-mesh sieve into a small bowl or Pyrex measuring cup. Using the back of a spoon, press the leaves against the strainer to ensure all the butter goes through the strainer. Discard the tea. Measure out ¾ cup of the butter and set aside. Use the excess to grease and flour a decorative 10-cup Bundt pan.

Next, put the eggs and sugars in the blender container and blend for 20 seconds.

Add the dry ingredients and pulse one or two times. Finally, add the buttermilk, vanilla, and butter; pulse two or three more times, until the mixture is just thoroughly combined. Use a rubber spatula to scrape down the sides of the container. Do not overmix. If the dry ingredients are not completely incorporated, stir a few times with the spatula.

Pour the batter into the prepared pan and bake for 40 to 50 minutes, or until a toothpick inserted into the center of the cake comes out clean. If the top of the cake starts to become a dark brown color after 40 minutes of baking, but the center is not yet set, cover the cake with foil while it finishes baking.

Let the cake cool in the Bundt pan for 15 minutes; then turn it out onto a rack set over waxed paper to cool for 1 hour.

Meanwhile, make the brown sugar glaze: Place the brown sugar, buttermilk, butter, and chai tea in a saucepan and cook over medium heat, stirring constantly, until the sugar has dissolved and the mixture just begins to boil. Remove from the heat and slowly drizzle the glaze over the cake, allowing it to run down the sides. Alternatively, skip the glaze and dust the cake with confectioners' sugar before serving.

Chocolate Coffee Quinoa Cookies

makes 2½ **dozen**

Along with its many other attributes, the blender works well as a spice and coffee grinder. Whole beans are ground in seconds by blender blades. Here ground coffee is added to a quinoa cookie with melty chocolate chips for a winning combination. Quinoa flour, which you can also grind in the blender (page 42) gives these gluten-free cookies a bit of a nutty, earthy flavor too.

¾ cup coconut oil, melted

¾ cup firmly packed dark brown sugar,

2 large eggs

⅓ cup almond butter

1 tablespoon pure vanilla extract

1¾ cups quinoa flour

½ teaspoon baking soda

½ teaspoon baking powder

½ teaspoon kosher salt

3 tablespoons ground coffee beans

1 cup old-fashioned rolled oats

1 cup bittersweet chocolate chips

3 tablespoons ground coffee beans

Preheat the oven to 350 degrees. Line two baking sheets with parchment paper. Put the coconut oil, brown sugar, eggs, almond butter and vanilla extract in the blender jar and process on medium for 20 seconds.

Add the quinoa flour, baking soda and powder, and salt. Run on medium for 5 seconds then increase the speed to high for 15 to 20 more seconds or until just combined. Use a spatula to scrape down the sides as needed.

Next, stir in the oats, chocolate chips and ground coffee. Using a tablespoon measure, scoop mounds of dough onto the prepared baking sheet about 2 inches apart. Bake for 8 minutes. The cookies may look underbaked but they will firm up as they cool. Allow the cookies to cool on the baking sheet for 5 minutes before transferring them to a wire rack to cool.

Easy Whipped Cream

makes 1½ cups

Literally, you can have lush heavenly whipped cream in under 2 minutes using the blender (that is, if you have all your ingredients readily on hand . . . it could take you longer to maneuver the vanilla out of the back of the cupboard!). Before my blender infatuation, I always turned to my stand mixer for whipping cream. I never even considered my tall, trusty friend. (I have yet to give it a name; it's still just my reliable unfailing Blender.) Well, folks, Blender does the job, and quite nicely I might say. No splattering cream. No waiting around. It's done before you can even think too much about it. Give it a whirl.

1½ cups cold heavy cream
1 tablespoon confectioners' sugar
1 teaspoon pure vanilla extract

Put the cream in the blender jar and process on medium for 20 seconds. Turn the power to high and blend for another 20 seconds.

Add the sugar and vanilla and blend on high until the cream is thick and fluffy and will hold soft peaks. Push the ingredients toward the blade with a spatula if necessary to ensure that the cream blends evenly. Serve immediately.

Roasted Strawberry Ice Cream

makes about 1 quart

It may seem counterintuitive to roast something that's being put into ice cream, but there's actually good reason. Roasting strawberries intensifies their flavor, and because the sugars begin to caramelize, it prevents the fruit from freezing rock-solid when blended into ice cream. Serve this with a few fresh berries on the side.

1 quart strawberries, hulled and cut in half

1 tablespoon organic cane sugar

1 (14-ounce) can sweetened condensed milk

1 cup whole milk

½ teaspoon pure vanilla extract

Preheat the oven to 375°F. Place the strawberries cut-side down on a parchment-lined baking sheet. Sprinkle with the cane sugar and roast for 25 minutes. Allow the strawberries to cool, then cover them and place the baking sheet in the freezer.

Once the berries are completely frozen, put them in the blender and add both milks and the vanilla. Pulse several times.

Transfer the mixture to a plastic container and refreeze, or freeze in an ice cream maker according to the manufacturer's instructions.

Just Bananas
Ice Cream

makes 2½ cups

Could dessert get any easier than this? Inspired by Eve Schaub, the author of A Year of No Sugar *(Source-books, 2014), this dessert is, as the name implies, just bananas. Eve and her family embarked on a year without sugar, which she writes about so entertainingly in the aforementioned book. Frozen banana ice cream was one of the desserts they savored during that time.*

6 bananas

Cut the bananas into 1-inch-thick slices and spread in a single layer on a parchment-lined baking sheet. Freeze for several hours or until frozen through.

Put all the frozen bananas in the blender container and run on medium until the mixture just becomes smooth. The bananas will first become crumbly, then will start to become smooth. It takes a few minutes, and you'll need to press the mixture toward the blade using a spatula several times.

If the amount seems too much for your machine, divide the bananas in half and blend. Running your blender on low also helps process the bananas. Be careful not to overwork your machine during the process. Serve immediately or refreeze if the mixture becomes too soft when blending. Top banana ice cream with ground nutmeg or cinnamon, granola, or toasted coconut.

Cherrylicious Frozen Yogurt

makes about 1 quart

This is one of those recipes where the beauty of the blender is especially apparent. Dessert in seconds, literally. You can eat this creamy cherry-yogurt combination straight from the blender, or put it in an ice cream maker for a slightly firmer texture. You can also switch up the fruits. Try other frozen berries and replace the almond extract with vanilla.

1 pound sweet cherries, pitted and frozen (about 3½ cups)

1½ cups Greek yogurt

¼ cup raw honey

1 teaspoon almond extract

Place all the ingredients in the blender and run for about 20 seconds.

Eat immediately, freeze in an ice cream maker according to the manufacturer's instructions, or place in the freezer to firm up.

Sweet Peach Ice Cream with Glazed Pecans

makes about 1 quart

Fresh peaches are the star here, with supporting roles played by the maple syrup, cinnamon, and pecans, which could take the lead given the chance. Their salty-sweet glaze makes them hard to resist.

For the ice cream

1 pound fresh peaches, peeled, cut into pieces, and frozen

4 egg yolks

1 cup coconut milk

2 tablespoons maple syrup

½ teaspoon ground cinnamon

For the Glazed Pecans

2 tablespoons unsalted butter

1 tablespoon dark brown sugar

1 cup pecan halves

½ teaspoon cinnamon

Pinch of kosher salt

To make the ice cream: Put all the ingredients in the blender and run on medium for about 20 seconds. Transfer the mixture to a plastic container and refreeze, or freeze in an ice cream maker according to the manufacturer's instructions.

To prepare the nuts: Preheat the oven to 350°F. Melt the butter and brown sugar in a skillet over medium heat. Add the pecans and cook, stirring constantly, for about 3 minutes.

Transfer the pecans to a parchment-lined baking sheet, spreading them evenly. Bake for 5 minutes or until golden brown. Cool completely, sprinkle on the ice cream, and enjoy!

Acknowledgments

This book emerged out of a lunch between two sixth graders one winter day—Susie and Camilla, who love to bake—and their moms, one with a belief in blenders, and the other who loves to blend. Girls, thanks for including us moms.

I'd like to extend a huge thank-you to my diligent and discerning testers: Janet Balletto, Sarah Brainard, Linda Dubilier, Michele Funccius Roszko, Jennifer Hall, Jennie Hartman, Charlotte Haukedal, Camilla Kampevold, Joanne Konrath, Babs Mansfield, Amoreena O'Bryon, Michelle Perreault-Dougherty, and Kaia Smithback. Your feedback is priceless.

I would also like to thank Marcey Brownstein for kindly loaning me her beautiful kitchenware, and Peter Appelson for supplying me with gorgeous surfaces (and beloved set of silverware!). I would also like to acknowledge Migliorelli Farmstand for its outstanding produce and good-natured spirit. Thanks also to Eve Schaub for inspiring me to eat less sugar.

To Maya, Seiya, and Julia for drinking milk, all kinds, again and again!

I am especially grateful to Kyle and Nile for their enthusiastic taste testing and recipe-naming efforts.

I would also like to give a special shout-out to Peter Bosch, who did what friends do: you helped me out in a time of need.

I am forever indebted to Michael and Judith Rosenthal for graciously opening their doors, literally, even when they weren't home. I am so grateful the stars have brought us together in our cherished locale. And I'll be forever thankful to the Reisses, whose friendship and generosity I deeply treasure.

I thank my mom and dad for their endless support, for allowing me to experiment in the kitchen when I was young, and showing me by example the value of family and meals shared together.

I am also grateful to my sister Lisa, for her willingness to test and make a mess, which is so unlike her, and letting me blend endlessly at the beach. A tremendous thanks to my entire extended family who taste-tested repeatedly while on vacation,—even little Henrik, who tried the soup.

I'd like to extend a big thanks to the Countryman Press team, including Michael Levatino, Anne Somlyo, and especially LeAnna Weller Smith for her beautiful work (and patience), and to Sarah Bennett, for all she does.

An especially huge thanks to Ann Treistman for her blender vision. You amaze me with your insight, passion, and thoroughness; not really sure how you do all you do—and you're such a pleasure to work with.

I am forever indebted to my star agent, Sharon Bowers, for her exceptional guidance. I adore you for many things, including your wicked sense of humor.

Annie Kamin, I truly appreciate that you stepped in and did what it takes to get things done; many thanks. Nina Weithorn, I am wowed by your culinary knowledge, hard work, and enchanting smile.

And to the profoundly talented Justin Lanier, who was my collaborator and partner in crime. You know I will always carry a special place in my heart for you. I thank you for making my vision a reality with your skill and determination. And an infinite amount of thanks goes to my family, who stood by me every step (or whir) along the way. To my brilliant and beautiful girls Anna and Camilla: I thank you for your willingness to try all things blended, to model and help on set, and to care—for others and the world around you. And I thank my dearest Jim for his unconditional love, support, and wit. I admire you greatly. You make my heart smile 24/7.

Index